Blood-Stained Hands
Past Atrocities in Kabul and Afghanistan's Legacy of Impunity

Human Rights Watch

#60931477

12-6-05

Human Rights Watch

350 Fifth Avenue, 34th floor
New York, NY 10118-3299 USA
Tel: 1-(212) 290-4700, Fax: 1-(212) 736-1300
hrwnyc@hrw.org

1630 Connecticut Avenue, N.W., Suite 500
Washington, DC 20009 USA
Tel:1-(202) 612-4321, Fax:1-(202) 612-4333
hrwdc@hrw.org

2nd Floor, 2-12 Pentonville Road
London N1 9HF, UK
Tel: 44 20 7713 1995, Fax: 44 20 7713 1800
hrwuk@hrw.org

Rue Van Campenhout 15,
1000 Brussels, Belgium
Tel: 32 (2) 732-2009, Fax: 32 (2) 732-0471
hrwatcheu@skynet.be

9 rue Cornavin
1201 Geneva
Tel: + 41 22 738 04 81, Fax: + 41 22 738 17 91
hrwgva@hrw.org

Web Site Address: http://www.hrw.org

Listserv address: To receive Human Rights Watch news releases by email, subscribe to
the HRW news listserv of your choice by visiting http://hrw.org/act/subscribe-
mlists/subscribe.htm

Human Rights Watch is dedicated to protecting the human rights of people around the world.

We stand with victims and activists to prevent discrimination, to uphold political freedom, to protect people from inhumane conduct in wartime, and to bring offenders to justice.

We investigate and expose human rights violations and hold abusers accountable.

We challenge governments and those who hold power to end abusive practices and respect international human rights law.

We enlist the public and the international community to support the cause of human rights for all.

HUMAN RIGHTS WATCH

Human Rights Watch conducts regular, systematic investigations of human rights abuses in some seventy countries around the world. Our reputation for timely, reliable disclosures has made us an essential source of information for those concerned with human rights. We address the human rights practices of governments of all political stripes, of all geopolitical alignments, and of all ethnic and religious persuasions. Human Rights Watch defends freedom of thought and expression, due process and equal protection of the law, and a vigorous civil society; we document and denounce murders, disappearances, torture, arbitrary imprisonment, discrimination, and other abuses of internationally recognized human rights. Our goal is to hold governments accountable if they transgress the rights of their people.

Human Rights Watch began in 1978 with the founding of its Europe and Central Asia division (then known as Helsinki Watch). Today, it also includes divisions covering Africa, the Americas, Asia, and the Middle East. In addition, it includes three thematic divisions on arms, children's rights, and women's rights. It maintains offices in Brussels, Geneva, London, Los Angeles, Moscow, New York, San Francisco, Tashkent, Toronto, and Washington. Human Rights Watch is an independent, nongovernmental organization, supported by contributions from private individuals and foundations worldwide. It accepts no government funds, directly or indirectly.

Blood-Stained Hands
Past Atrocities in Kabul and Afghanistan's Legacy of Impunity

We went to Kabul with a lot of glory and pride. . . . [W]e were encouraged that our country would lead forward, gain strength, and we would stand on our own two feet. The recent attacks on Kabul have shattered all the hopes of the Afghan people and caused us tremendous humiliation in the international community.

—Hamid Karzai, deputy foreign minister, to the Associated Press, August 23, 1992.

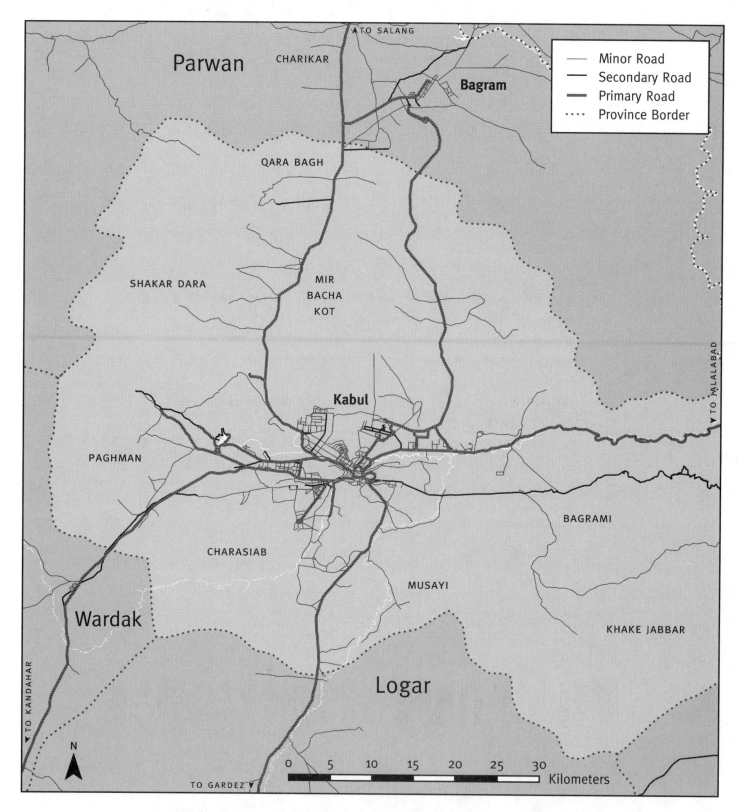

Kabul Province and Surrounding Areas

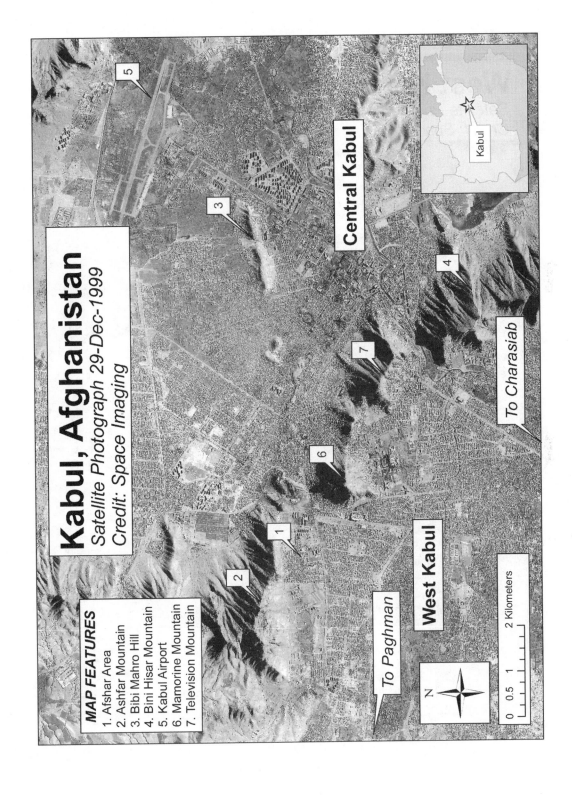

Kabul, Afghanistan
Satellite Photograph 29-Dec-1999
Credit: Space Imaging

MAP FEATURES
1. Afshar Area
2. Ashfar Mountain
3. Bibi Mahro Hill
4. Bini Hisar Mountain
5. Kabul Airport
6. Mamorine Mountain
7. Television Mountain

Central Kabul

West Kabul

To Charasiab

To Paghman

N

0   0.5   1   2 Kilometers

Kabul

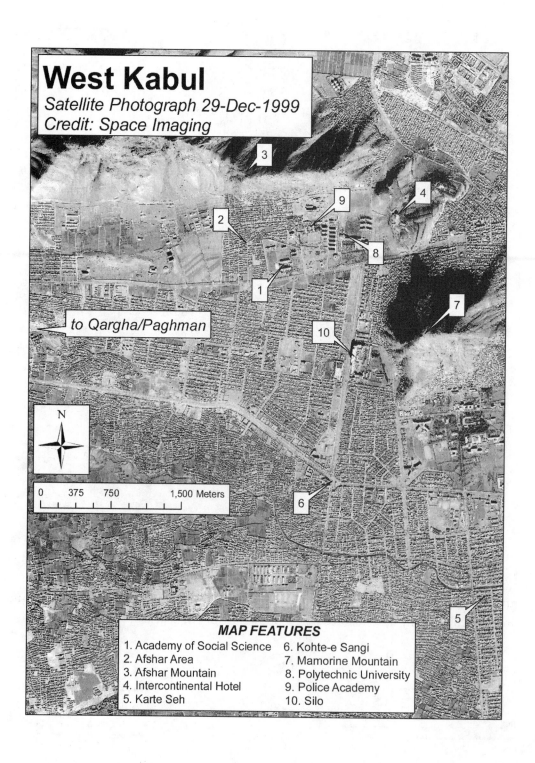

West Kabul
Satellite Photograph 29-Dec-1999
Credit: Space Imaging

3

9

2

4

8

1

7

to Qargha/Paghman

10

N

0   375   750   1,500 Meters

6

5

MAP FEATURES
1. Academy of Social Science   6. Kohte-e Sangi
2. Afshar Area   7. Mamorine Mountain
3. Afshar Mountain   8. Polytechnic University
4. Intercontinental Hotel   9. Police Academy
5. Karte Seh   10. Silo

I. Introduction

Afghanistan has suffered from over two decades of war. This is the typical opening of most reports, articles, and speeches written about Afghanistan today. The statement, usually used to help explain the country's post-Taliban challenges, is repeated so frequently that it has become a cliché. Yet few efforts have been made to study the history itself and its significance for Afghanistan's current situation. More remarkable, despite the fact the two-decade period was marked by widespread human rights abuses, war crimes, and crimes against humanity, the statement is rarely followed by suggestions that perpetrators of past crimes, most of whom are still alive, should be brought to justice. Afghanistan's past is often invoked, but rarely addressed.

This report, which documents only one short part of that two-decade past, is not an attempt to remedy the situation. This report is not a comprehensive history of armed conflict in Afghanistan over the last two decades or a full accounting of the crimes of this period. Nor could it be. Complete documentation of the most serious atrocities committed in Afghanistan in the 1980s and 1990s, when it is accomplished, will require broad-based and long-term efforts backed fully by both the Afghan government and the international community. When such a history is written, it will not fit within the covers of a book; it will fill bookshelves.

Rather, this report focuses on a single year in Afghanistan's history: the Afghan year of 1371 (April 1992 to March 1993), immediately succeeding the collapse of the Soviet-backed government in Kabul. It also focuses on events in a single place: Afghanistan's capital, Kabul, and its immediate environs.

Why Kabul, and why 1371? To start, there is the scale of the abuses and their context. The year 1371 was Afghanistan's first full year of freedom from Soviet manipulation, in the wake of ten years of Soviet occupation in the 1980s. The change of power in Kabul in 1371 could easily have marked a new beginning for Afghanistan.

Instead, it was one of its darkest eras. As this report shows, Kabul in 1371 was the scene of almost constant armed conflict among hostile Afghan military factions—rival mujahedin forces and defecting army forces who swept into the city after the Soviet-backed government collapsed. During this period, the various factions battled over Kabul and committed countless atrocities against the Afghan civilian population. Tens of thousands of civilians were killed and injured amidst the fighting. Many if not most of these civilian casualties were the result of direct or indiscriminate attacks on the civilian population and other serious violations of international humanitarian law (the laws of war). Militias abducted thousands of civilians during this period; most were never seen again. Much of the city was looted and destroyed. Most of the destruction that scars Kabul even today took place during this period and in the years immediately following—before the Taliban marched on Kabul.

The crimes of this period have not received as much attention as crimes committed during other phases of Afghanistan's wars. The whole history of conflict in Afghanistan from the Soviet invasion to the present was marked by atrocities. In the 1980s (Afghan years 1359-68), the Soviet Red Army and its allied Afghan army committed massive war crimes and crimes against humanity, intentionally targeting civilians and civilian areas for attack, killing prisoners, and torturing and murdering detainees. And in the mid- to late-1990s (Afghan years 1375-1380), the Taliban committed numerous war crimes during military operations, and as a governing power operated almost entirely outside of established human rights standards.

Human Rights Watch and other human rights groups have already documented, in numerous earlier reports, the atrocities of Soviet armed forces and the Afghan client government, and the crimes and repression of the Taliban in the 1990s. In addition, the United Nations has compiled an index of war crimes, crimes against humanity, and human rights violations during the entire period from 1978 to 2001, focusing largely on Soviet and Taliban abuses (this report was never publicly released, but was supplied to the Afghan government in January 2005). Abuses from the Soviet and Taliban periods have also been covered widely in international media.

The early 1990s, however, including the Afghan year 1371, have received relatively little attention. Internationally, this period was overshadowed by other events, including the U.S. presidential campaign between Bill Clinton and George H.W. Bush in 1992, the breakup of the Soviet Union, and war in the former Yugoslavia. In the United States, the fall of the Soviet-backed regime in late April 1992 was upstaged by violent race riots in Los Angeles, California.

Generally, little information is available today about what happened in Afghanistan during 1371. A relatively small number of Afghan and international journalists covered events during this period, and media editors and producers often passed on the stories journalists filed. There were no functioning Afghan news services. No international human rights monitors were deployed in the country at the time, few humanitarian groups were operating, and there was only a modest United Nations presence with no direct mandate to report on the human rights situation. This report attempts to fill some of these informational gaps.

A second reason for our focus on the early 1990s lies in this period's specific relevance to the present. Many of the main commanders and political faction leaders implicated in the crimes detailed in this report are now officials in the Afghan government—serving in high level positions in the police, military, intelligence services, and even as advisors to President Hamid Karzai. Others may be actively seeking such positions. Many Afghans, and Kabulis in particular, believe that these leaders' history of abuse makes them unsuitable to hold such positions.

We agree. Human Rights Watch has been working in conflict and post-conflict settings in four continents for over twenty-five years. We have observed the successes and failures of numerous peace-building processes, and documented time after time how post-conflict leaders with records of past abuse—with their penchant for resolving political issues through force instead of law—have continued to commit abuses and allowed lawlessness to persist or return.

These lessons are applicable in Afghanistan today. Despite the 2001 Bonn Agreement, which established a government under President Karzai, most parts of Afghanistan are still controlled by autonomous commanders—warlords—who control militia factions of varying sizes and continue to threaten the country's peace-building efforts. Many of these warlords and factions, named in this report as being implicated in past abuses, have been involved in contemporary human rights abuses in the Kabul area since 2001, including looting of homes, abduction, torture of detainees, rape, and murder.

Human Rights Watch has documented much of this abuse in past reports.[1] Many high level officials named in this report, and in our past reports, have also been implicated in widespread land-grabbing schemes in reports by the Afghan Independent Human Rights Commission (AIHRC).

Simply put, many of the warlords involved in abuses in the early 1990s are repeat offenders. This pattern of recidivism is common sense to many Kabulis, many of whom have repeatedly told Human Rights Watch over the last three years: "*Jangsalaran jangsalar hastand.*" ("Warlords are [and remain] warlords.") But the lesson seems to be lost on many Afghan and international officials.

---

[1] See, e.g., Human Rights Watch, *"Killing You is a Very Easy Thing For Us": Human Rights Abuses in Southeast Afghanistan*, A Human Rights Watch Short Report, vol. 15, no. 5 (C), July 2003, available at http://www.hrw.org/reports/2003/afghanistan0703; and Human Rights Watch, *Paying for the Taliban's Crimes: Abuses Against Ethnic Pashtuns in Northern Afghanistan*, A Human Rights Watch Short Report, vol. 14, no. 2(c), n. 13, available at http://www.hrw.org/reports/2002/afghan2.

Specific Findings

This report documents numerous serious human rights abuses, war crimes, and crimes against humanity that occurred from April 1992—the collapse of the government of President Najibullah, the leader once backed by the Soviet Union—to March 1993.

Section II, following this introduction, provides an historical background to the events of that year. Section III (A) details the capture of Kabul by various anti-Najibullah mujahedin forces in late April 1992, and describes violence in the city from April through December of 1992 as these forces began to fight among themselves. The report documents the different abuses committed by each of the factions during this period, including indiscriminate military attacks, intentional targeting of civilians, murders and assaults on civilians, abductions, forced labor, and looting of civilian homes. It also discusses allegations that members of particular factions raped women as well as girls and boys.

In section III (B), the report documents how fighting intensified in January 1993. Section III (C) describes how that fighting culminated in the February 1993 Afshar campaign—a military attack by various mujahedin forces against Shi'a mujahedin forces in the west of the city. As the report shows, in the lead-up to the attack, hundreds of people were killed in indiscriminate or intentional attacks on civilian homes, and thousands more were displaced. As documented here, militias murdered scores of civilians in front of their homes during the attack. Hundreds more were abducted and never seen again.

In section IV, we discuss the legal culpability of various factions and leaders for their involvement in the documented abuses, including numerous commanders who hold positions in Afghanistan's government as of mid-2005.

Section V sets forth detailed recommendations.

The Responsible Parties

As shown below, the factions and leaders involved in the documented abuses include:

- *Jamiat-e Islami-yi Afghanistan* (hereafter "Jamiat"), a predominately Tajik faction led politically by Burhanuddin Rabbani and commanded militarily by Ahmad Shah Massoud (killed in a suicide attack on September 9, 2001).

- *Shura-e Nazar*, a federation of military forces led by various mujahedin commanders, mostly from the north and northeast of Afghanistan, united under Massoud's military command.

- *Hezb-e Islami*, a predominately Pashtun faction under the command of Gulbuddin Hekmatyar, and one of the primary recipients of military assistance from the United States and Pakistan through the 1980s and early 1990s.

- *Ittihad-i Islami Bara-yi Azadi Afghanistan* (hereafter "Ittihad"), a predominately Pashtun faction headed by Abdul Rabb al-Rasul Sayyaf, linked to and supported by Saudi Arabia.

- *Hezb-e Wahdat-e Islami-yi Afghanistan* (hereafter "Wahdat"), the principal Shi'a and predominately Hazara faction in Afghanistan led in 1992-1993 by Abdul Ali Mazari (killed in 1996) and heavily supported by Iran.

- *Junbish-e Milli-yi Islami-yi Afghanistan* (hereafter "Junbish"), a predominately Uzbek and Turkmen militia, based in northern Afghanistan, led by Abdul Rashid Dostum (a general in the Soviet-backed Afghan army during the 1980s) and comprised of forces from the former Soviet-backed army and various mujahedin militias from the north of the country.

- *Harakat-e Islami-yi Afghanistan* (hereafter "Harakat"), a predominately Shi'a faction headed politically by Mohammad Asef Mohseni and militarily by Hossein Anwari, supported by Iran.

During most of the period discussed in this report, the sovereignty of Afghanistan was vested formally in "The Islamic State of Afghanistan," an entity created in April 1992, after the fall of the Soviet-backed Najibullah government. This government was headed from April to June 1992 by Sibghatullah Mujaddidi, a relatively weak political leader from a small mujahedin party in Peshawar, chosen to be president as a compromise by most (but not all) of the parties named above. For the remaining period covered in this report, and until the Taliban entered Kabul in 1996, the presidency was held by Burhanuddin Rabbani, the political leader of Jamiat.

With the exception of Hekmatyar's Hezb-e Islami, all of the parties listed above were ostensibly unified under this government in April 1992 (but as described below, Wahdat later changed sides, in late 1992, and allied with Hezb-e Islami). The military, police, and intelligence forces loosely organized under this government were, at least at the beginning of the period covered in this report, comprised mostly of Jamiat and Junbish troops, although these militias also allied with soldiers from the Ittihad, Wahdat, and Harakat factions. Commanders and officials from the Jamiat, Junbish, and Ittihad parties often met at the office of the president and Ministry of Defense to coordinate.

Hekmatyar's Hezb-e Islami, for its part, refused to recognize the government for most of the period discussed in this report and launched attacks against government forces and Kabul generally. (Mazari's Wahdat forces joined in these efforts in late 1992.)

As shown in this report, each of these forces in 1992-1993 had hierarchical military structures with a chief commander, sub-commanders at various levels, and soldiers.[2] These hierarchies made it possible for factional leaders and commanders to have effective control over subordinates, and leaders and commanders could order troops to act, and not to act, and ensure that troops would obey. These hierarchies were not always transparent or consistent—and complicated ethnic, tribal, and family relations

---

[2] Descriptions of factions' command structures in this report are based on numerous interviews with sources familiar with the events of 1992-1993, including Afghan humanitarian workers, journalists, historians, and government officials; international aid workers, health workers, journalists, and diplomats; and mujahedin and other factional leaders. The command structures of these factions are also discussed in detail in section IV. For a broader analysis of various mujahedin parties in the early 1990s acknowledging and describing their command structures, see Barnett R. Rubin, *The Search for Peace in Afghanistan: From Buffer State to Failed State* (New Haven: Yale, 1995) pp. 117-119; Amin Saikal, "The Rabbani Government, 1992-1996" in *Fundamentalism Reborn? Afghanistan and the Taliban* (William Maley, ed., Lahore: Vanguard Books, 1998), pp. 34-36; Noor Mohammed Sangar, *Neem Negahi Bar E'telafhay-e Tanzimi dar Afghanistan* ("*A Brief Glance at Factional Alliances in Afghanistan*") (Peshawar: publisher unknown, 2003); and Tschanguiz Pahlavan, *Afghanistan: The Era of Mujahedeen and the Rise of the Taliban* (Tehran: Ghatreh Publishing House, 1999).

made the command structures fluid. But the groups were organized, and commanders in many respects did control troops. Many of the atrocities and abuses documented in this report were avoidable, not unstoppable. Some abuses, as shown below, may have been directly ordered by commanders.

For more information on the make-up and characteristics of the factions listed above, see Appendix A.

The Value of Justice

Everyone has blood on their hands. This is another oft-repeated phrase about Afghanistan. For many Afghans, it is an indictment: a denunciation of the warlords in Afghanistan's current government with past records of abuse and war crimes. Many if not most Afghans hated the cruelty and viciousness of Taliban rule. But Afghans also remember the period before their rule, when many of Afghanistan's current military and political leadership were in Kabul, serving as factional commanders or officials in the erstwhile government. They remember how the factions looted and fought bloody street battles throughout Kabul, typically with total disregard to their effect on the civilian population. And they also remember the Soviet period, with its terrible crimes.

However, for many Afghan and international officials, *Everyone has blood on their hands* is an excuse: a justification for inaction in holding some of the world's most serious human rights offenders accountable for their crimes. "No one has clean hands," officials sometime say, referring to Afghanistan's potential leaders, a statement that disregards the millions of Afghans inside and outside the country who never took part in Afghanistan's hostilities.

There are literally millions of Afghans without "blood on their hands." And many of them would be eligible to serve as officials in Afghanistan's government, or run for office. Some have, and have served with distinction. Yet many qualified Afghans are today afraid of taking part in governance, fearful of more powerful militia leaders whose hands, they say in Dari, "*be khoon agheshteh hast*"—are indeed stained with blood.

The truth is that most Afghans want these factional commanders and officials involved in this fighting to be held accountable for the crimes committed during this period—along with those involved in Soviet-era and Taliban-era abuses. The Afghan Independent Human Rights Commission completed a survey in 2004, based on in-depth interviews and focus groups with thousands of Afghans across the country, focusing on citizens' views on past crimes and what to do about addressing them. The findings made it clear that the vast majority of Afghans want the crimes of the past to be confronted. This is not surprising, given the extent to which the Afghan population has been affected by conflict. As the commission noted in the report:

> The atrocities that were committed in Afghanistan are of an enormous scale, and the sense of victimization among the people we spoke to is widespread and profound. Almost everyone had been touched by violence in some way. When we asked 4,151 respondents as part of the survey whether they had been personally affected by violations during the conflict, 69 percent identified themselves or their immediate families as direct victims of a serious human rights violation during the 23-year period. Out of over 2,000 focus group participants, over 500 referred to killings among their relatives. Almost 400 had experienced torture or detention either themselves or in their immediate family. These are staggering statistics, in comparison to any other conflict in the world.[3]

According to the AIHRC survey results, 94 percent of Afghans consider justice for past crimes to be either "very important" (75.9 percent) or "important" (18.5 percent). When asked what the effects would be for Afghanistan in bringing war criminals to justice, 76 percent said it would "increase stability and bring security," and only 7.6 percent said it would "decrease stability and threaten security." Almost half of those questioned said war criminals should be brought to justice "now," and another 25 percent said perpetrators should be tried "within two years."[4]

Human Rights Watch, along with numerous other international and Afghan non-governmental organizations, has repeatedly called on Afghan officials and international actors involved in Afghanistan to help organize independent and impartial mechanisms to hold accountable persons responsible for war crimes and serious human rights abuses committed since 1978, and we fully agree with the AIHRC on the need for this issue to receive more attention.

The AIHRC has also made a number of recommendations for moving forward, including short-term and immediate measures for sidelining past abusers from government service ("vetting"), building up the capacity for criminal trials, and exploring options for reparations and compensation for victims.

---

[3] Afghan Independent Human Rights Commission, "A Call for Justice: A Report on National Consultations on Transitional Justice in Afghanistan," January 2005.

[4] Ibid.

Human Rights Watch in general supports the AIHRC's recommendations (see section V, below), especially on the need for vetting government officials and rebuilding the judicial system to allow for fair trials of those implicated in serious international crimes.

In short, we agree with the majority of Afghans—and the AIHRC—that justice for past crimes in Afghanistan is important, and that ongoing impunity is damaging efforts to develop Afghanistan and reestablish the rule of law.

Continued impunity is an affront not only to the victims of past abuse, but to all Afghans, and a stumbling block on the road to Afghanistan's peaceful future. The purpose of this report, among other things, is to help pressure the Afghan government and international community to take action to address this impunity, so that Afghans get what they want: justice.

As an immediate first step, we recommend that the government implement a set of vetting processes for government officials. We also recommend that immediate efforts be taken to accelerate judicial reform. We further recommend that the government work to create a Special Court to try past offenders, and that the court be comprised of both Afghan and international judges, with an international majority, and that the prosecutor's office be led by an international prosecutor.

A complete recommendations section appears on page 125.

Methodology of this report

This report is based on over 150 in-depth interviews with witnesses and victims of abuses in 1992-1993 and faction members and officials familiar with events at the time. Those interviewed include civilians in Kabul during the fighting, Afghan and international print, radio, and television journalists who ventured through Kabul during the hostilities, health workers at Kabul's hospitals, government and factional officials and troops, among others. Human Rights Watch has also interviewed military experts and analysts familiar with mujahedin groups and the weapons systems and military tactics these groups used in 1992-1993.

In most cases, Afghan and international sources interviewed by Human Rights Watch voiced serious concern about their ongoing security, given the sensitivity of the issues and the continuing power of some of the persons implicated in the abuses discussed. For these reasons, most sources are identified by initials (e.g., "G.H.K.") which are not associated with their actual name.

The use of ethnic group identifications in this report does not constitute endorsement or approval of the use of ethnically based distinctions in identifying Afghan citizens. Many Afghans share more than one ethnic ancestry or are intermarried. Still, most Afghans identify themselves as belonging to a single particular ethnic group—usually their fathers'. Except where otherwise stated, all references to Afghans' ethnic identities (for instance, Tajik, Pashtun, Uzbek, Hazara) and religious identities (Sunni and Shi'a) are based on interviewees' own identifications.

II. Historical Background

Before it all started, the city was very much intact. It was surprising to me that it was so intact. Afterwards, of course, it was all destroyed.

—Jeremy Bowen, correspondent with the British Broadcasting Corporation (BBC), discussing fighting in Kabul between mujahedin factions after the fall of the Soviet-backed government in 1992.[5]

The history of modern armed conflict in Afghanistan began in April 1978, when Soviet-backed Afghan communists took control of the government in a coup, overthrowing the president of Afghanistan, Muhammad Daoud Khan, the cousin of Afghanistan's former king, Zahir Shah, who was earlier overthrown in a bloodless coup by Daoud in 1973.[6]

The "Saur Revolution" (named for the Afghan calendar month when it occurred) went badly from the start. The communists who seized power in Kabul consisted of two opposed political parties—Khalq and Parcham.[7] Each had little popular support, especially outside of Kabul and other main cities, and many segments of the country's army and police opposed the coup.

The new government soon came to be dominated by a ruthless Khalq leader, Hafizullah Amin, who sought to create a communist economy in Afghanistan virtually overnight through purges, arrests, and terror. An insurgency was launched against the new regime,

---

[5] Human Rights Watch telephone interview with Jeremy Bowen, correspondent with the British Broadcasting Corporation in Kabul in 1992, April 12, 2004.

[6] For information about the periods discussed in this section, see Barnett R. Rubin, *The Fragmentation of Afghanistan: State Formation and Collapse in the International System*, Second Edition (New Haven: Yale, 2002) and Rubin, *The Search for Peace in Afghanistan*; Olivier Roy, *Islam and Resistance in Afghanistan* (Cambridge: Cambridge University Press, 1986); and Steve Coll, *Ghost Wars: The Secret History of the CIA, Afghanistan, and Bin Laden, from the Soviet Invasion to September 10, 2001* (New York: Penguin, 2004). See also Mohammad Nabi Azimi, *Ordu va Siyasat Dar Seh Daheh Akheer-e Afghanistan ("Army and Politics in the Last Three Decades in Afghanistan")* (Peshawar: Marka-e Nashrati Mayvand, 1998); Sangar, *Neem Negahi Bar E'telafhay-e Tanzimi dar Afghanistan;* and Mir Agha Haghjoo, *Afghanistan va Modakhelat-e Khareji ("Afghanistan and Foreign Interferences")* (Tehran: Entesharat Majlesi, 2001).

[7] The names of the two parties derived from their respective newspapers, Khalq (the masses) and Parcham (the flag). At the time of the 1978 coup, Khalq and Parcham were ostensibly united within the People's Democratic Party of Afghanistan (PDPA).

and in 1979, the Soviet Union invaded Afghanistan to support the failing revolution and government, and installed a new leader from the Parcham party, Babrak Karmal.

But it was too late to put down the insurgency, which was already well-advanced and widespread. The rebels included former officers and troops of the Afghan military, members of exiled Islamist groups in Pakistan and Iran, and militias of numerous other disgruntled political groups. Loosely allied under a common theme—defenders of Islamic and Afghan values against Soviet occupation and ideology—these diverse parties enjoyed widespread support within and outside Afghanistan. They came to be known as "the mujahedin" and their battle as "the jihad."

There was never any real unity between the mujahedin parties: some were openly hostile and occasionally fought battles with each other. But for most of the 1980s, the mujahedin groups—with the indispensable support of the United States, as well as the United Kingdom, Saudi Arabia, China, Iran, and Pakistan—fought an effective and often brutal guerrilla war against Soviet and Afghan national forces, attacking convoys, patrols, arms depots, government offices, airfields, and even civilian areas. The Soviet and Afghan national armies, for their part, regularly attacked or bombed mujahedin bases and villages, and harshly suppressed mujahedin organization and other anti-government activities. Much of the countryside became a battle zone in the 1980s.

The war had terrible effects on civilian life in Afghanistan. Both sides regularly committed serious human rights abuses and violations of international humanitarian law. The Soviets often targeted civilians or civilian infrastructure for military attack, and government forces under their control brutally suppressed the civilian population. Mujahedin forces also committed abuses and violations, targeting civilians for attack and using illegal methods of warfare.[8] It is estimated that well over one million people were killed by conflict and violence during the Soviet occupation and over seven million people were displaced from their homes.[9]

---

[8] For more information on human rights abuses and violations of international humanitarian law during the Soviet occupation of Afghanistan, see Human Rights Watch, "Tears, Blood, and Cries: Human Rights in Afghanistan Since the Invasion, 1979 to 1984," *A Helsinki Watch and Asia Watch Report*, 1984; Human Rights Watch, "To Die in Afghanistan," *A Helsinki Watch and Asia Watch Report*, 1985; Human Rights Watch, "To Win the Children," *A Helsinki Watch and Asia Watch Report*, 1986; Human Rights Watch, "By All Parties to the Conflict," *A Helsinki Watch and Asia Watch Report*, 1988. See also, Jeri Laber and Barnett R. Rubin, *A Nation is Dying* (Illinois: Northwestern University Press, 1988); Amnesty International, *Afghanistan: Torture of Political Prisoners* (London: Amnesty International Publications, 1986).

[9] Rubin, *The Fragmentation of Afghanistan*, p. 1.

Militarily and financially exhausted, and spurred on by *perestroika*, the Soviet Union finally withdrew from Afghanistan in 1989. It continued to support the Kabul government, which was now headed by Najibullah, a former head of Afghanistan's Soviet-trained intelligence service, KHAD.[10]

The Afghan nation, however, had been shattered by communist rule and Soviet occupation. By 1989 approximately one-fifth of its population had fled abroad and much of Afghanistan's rural infrastructure was destroyed. The cohesion of the Afghan nation and concepts of national identity were severely compromised, and there were deep social, ethnic, religious, and political divisions within and between the existing regime and mujahedin parties.

The conflict also filled the country with weapons. Afghanistan was not particularly militarized in the late 1970s, when the communist coup took place. The mujahedin in 1979 were severely under-equipped to fight a standing Soviet army, and the communist Afghan government was severely disorganized and poorly outfitted. All that changed. In the 1980's, the United States and Saudi Arabia, and to a lesser extent Iran and China, allocated an estimated $6 to $12 billion dollars (U.S.) in military aid to mujahedin groups, while the Soviet Union sent approximately $36 to $48 billion of military aid into the country to support the government.[11] (Pakistan, where some of the mujahedin parties set up exile headquarters, arranged large military training programs for the mujahedin and controlled how much of the Saudi and U.S. assistance was delivered.) During the 1980's, Afghanistan likely received more light weapons than any other country in the world, and by 1992 it was estimated that there were more light weapons in Afghanistan than in India and Pakistan combined.[12]

Despite the Soviet withdrawal, through 1989-1991 battles between mujahedin and government forces continued. The mujahedin parties made few attempts at compromise, and Najibullah stubbornly refused to step down as his power eroded. The mujahedin—deeply divided with historical rivalries and religious, ethnic, and linguistic

---

[10] KHAD stands for *Khademat-e Ettela'at-e Dawlati* ("State Intelligence Service").

[11] See Larry P. Goodson, *Afghanistan's Endless War: State Failure, Regional Politics, and the Rise of the Taliban* (Seattle: University of Washington Press, 2001), pp. 63 and 99; Coll, *Ghost Wars*, pp. 65-66, 151, 190, and 239. See also generally, George Crile, *Charlie Wilson's War: The Extraordinary Story of the Largest Covert Operation in History* (New York: Atlantic Monthly Press, 2003); Human Rights Watch, *Crisis of Impunity: The Role of Pakistan, Russia, and Iran in Fueling the Civil War*, A Human Rights Watch Short Report, July 2001, vol. 13, no. 3 (C); Haghjoo, *Modakhelat-e Khareji*, pp. 106-160; and Mohammed Nabi Azimi, *Ordu va Siyasat*, pp. 225-325.

[12] See Rubin, *The Fragmentation of Afghanistan*, p. 196.

differences—also increasingly began to fight among themselves as they took more territory from the government. The U.S. government began to turn its attention away from Afghanistan, even as it, along with Pakistan, Saudi Arabia, and Iran, continued to arm mujahedin forces. The Soviet Union continued its support for Najibullah. There were few international efforts to mediate to prevent the increasing fragmentation of armed groups in Afghanistan. Peacemaking efforts were mostly put in the hands of the U.N. Secretary-General's office, which lacked the political clout to force the parties to compromise. The war—increasingly a multi-party civil war—went on.

A Soviet soldier in a military parade in Kabul marking the start of the pullout of Soviet forces from Afghanistan in 1988. © 1988 Robert Nickelsberg

President Najibullah, the last Soviet-backed leader of Afghanistan. Formerly the head of Afghanistan's Soviet-trained intelligence agency, KHAD, Najibullah retained power for four years after the Soviet withdrawal. He agreed to resign in March 1992, three months after the Soviet Union cut off assistance to his government. He was killed by the Taliban in 1996. © 1990 Robert Nickelsberg

The disunity among the mujahedin—a key obstacle to peace-making efforts—was aggravated throughout this period by the continuing policy of the United States, Pakistan, and Saudi Arabia to give a disproportionate amount of military assistance to one particular mujahedin party: the Hezb-e Islami of Gulbuddin Hekmatyar.[13] Through the 1980's, Hekmatyar received the majority of assistance from these countries, and in 1991, the CIA (with Pakistani support) was still channeling most U.S. assistance through Hekmatyar—including large shipments of Soviet weapons and tanks the United States captured in Iraq during the first Gulf War (weapons used by Hekmatyar later to attack Kabul in 1992-1996).[14] Unity among the different mujahedin groups was made especially difficult because of Hekmatyar's constant demands for a disproportionate share of power in a post-Najibullah government, and the resentment and hatred toward Hekmatyar in other parties, who believed they had fought against Soviet forces just as decisively as Hezb-e Islami (if not more) and with less assistance.[15] As the Soviet Union collapsed, there were increasing signs that the war it started in Afghanistan would last for a long time, even as the regime it supported collapsed.

*   *   *   *   *   *

In September 1991, the Soviet Union and the United States agreed to a reciprocal cut-off in funding and assistance to Najibullah's government and mujahedin forces respectively, starting January 1, 1992. At this point, it was clear to all parties that the government's days were numbered. Whole sections of Afghanistan, including areas on the Pakistan border, were already in the hands of mujahedin factions, and without Soviet support the Najibullah government's grip on Kabul was loosening.[16]

Mujahedin leaders, however, were still in disagreement about a post-Najibullah power-sharing plan. Through the spring of 1992, the United Nations, along with Saudi and Pakistani officials, worked with major Sunni and Shi'a parties to fashion an agreement.

---

[13] See Haghjoo, *Modakhelat-e Khareji*, pp. 168-189; for a broad discussion of the disunity among mujahedin groups, see Mohammed Zaher Azimi, *Afghanistan va Reeshey-e Dardha 1371-1377 ("Afghanistan and the Roots of the Misery 1992-1998")* (Peshawar: Markaz-e Nashrati Mayvand, 1998).

[14] See Coll, *Ghost Wars*, p. 226; and Steve Coll, "Afghan Rebels Said to Use Iraqi Tanks," *The Washington Post*, October 1, 1991.

[15] See Rubin, *The Fragmentation of Afghanistan*, pp. 196-201; Saikal, "The Rabbani Government, 1992-1996" in *Fundamentalism Reborn*, pp. 30-31.

[16] For more information on events in this specific period, see Rubin, *The Fragmentation of Afghanistan*, pp. 266-274, and *The Search for Peace in Afghanistan*, pp. 127-135; Saikal, "The Rabbani Government, 1992-1996" in *Fundamentalism Reborn*; M. Hassan Kakar, *Afghanistan: The Soviet Invasion and Afghan Response, 1979-1982* (Epilogue) (Berkeley and Los Angeles: University of California Press, 1995).

On March 18, 1992, under strong pressure from the United States and Pakistan (via the United Nations), Najibullah agreed to resign as head of state as soon as a transitional authority was formed. He appeared on Afghan television to make the announcement.[17] The next day, the government's main military leader in the north, General Rashid Dostum, defected from the government and agreed to form a coalition force with commanders from the Wahdat and Jamiat forces. This unified force then took control of the northern city of Mazar-e Sharif and surrounding areas.[18] With the border of Pakistan already held by other mujahedin forces, Kabul was now effectively surrounded.

As the Afghan New Year of 1371 began at the spring equinox—March 21, 1992—it was clear that the communist era was over in Afghanistan, but it was unclear whether 1371 would be peaceful. The government in Kabul stood, as the U.N. continued to try to work out a post-Najibullah power sharing plan.

On April 10, U.N. Secretary-General Boutros Boutros-Ghali presented a plan to the mujahedin parties, which they in turn approved, to form a "pre-transition council composed of impartial personalities" to accept formal sovereignty from Najibullah and then convene a *shura* (traditional Afghan council) in Kabul to choose an interim government.[19] The plan was for the U.N. to fly the council—mostly elder exiled community and tribal leaders—into Kabul the night of April 15 and then fly Najibullah out of the country to exile. Mujahedin parties would remain outside the city throughout.

On the ground, however, events were already in flux. Massoud's forces seized control of the Bagram airbase north of Kabul and much of the Shomali plain north of the capital, along with forces working for Dostum, who had now formed a new political-military party: Junbish-e Melli-ye Islami (the National Islamic Movement). Both forces were literally just outside Kabul. Hekmatyar, meanwhile, had moved Hezb-e Islami forces just to the south of the city.

---

[17] See Rubin, *The Search for Peace in Afghanistan*, p. 128.

[18] For a detailed discussion of the political background and details of the fall of Mazar-e Sharif, see Assadollah Wolwalji, *Safehat-e Shomal-e Afghanistan dar Fasseleh-e Beyn-e Tarh va Tahaghghogh-e Barnamey-e Khorooj-e Artesh-e Sorkh az een Keshvar ("What Occurred in the Northern Plains of Afghanistan During the Planning and Implementation of the Withdrawal of the Red Army from This Country")* (Unknown, likely Peshawar: Edareh-e Nashrati Golestan, 2001); see also Mohammed Nabi Azimi, *Ordu va Siyasat*, pp. 512-525 (regarding the conduct and views of the Afghan national armed forces in the north during this period).

[19] See U.N. Department of Public Information, "Statement of the Secretary-General on Afghanistan," April 10, 1992.

Government forces en masse were beginning to defect to the different mujahedin parties, offering assistance to each of the parties entering Kabul. Hekmatyar and Massoud had each worked to cultivate defectors among government security forces, and Dostum, as a former government official, already had links to officials in Kabul.

The dynamics of these defections were heavily influenced by ethnic identity. Most Pashtun officials and police officers in the interior ministry (mostly from the Khalq faction) now sought to build alliances with Hekmatyar, while Tajik officers in the military and government (mostly Parcham) were defecting to Massoud. Turkmen and Uzbek officials were siding with Dostum.

On April 15, as Najibullah prepared to resign, some mujahedin parties balked at the U.N. arrangement, undermining the agreement. That night, the chief U.N. mediator, Benon Sevan, flew alone to Kabul to pick up Najibullah. But as Najibullah approached the airport, his car was blocked by militia forces. Najibullah backtracked into the city and took refuge in the Kabul U.N. compound (where he was to remain for the next four years, until the Taliban took control and killed him).[20] Sevan flew back to Pakistan to continue negotiations. Meanwhile, Pashtun government officials in the interior and defense ministries were starting to allow forces from Hekmatyar's Hezb-e Islami party into the city, to prepare for his entrance into the city. Massoud and Dostum remained north of the city while mujahedin representatives continued to work on a power-sharing agreement in Peshawar.

On April 24, as Hekmatyar was about to seize control of the city, Massoud and Dostum's forces entered Kabul, taking control of most government ministries. Jamiat and Junbish attacked Hezb-e Islami forces occupying the interior ministry and Presidential Palace, pushing Hezb-e Islami south and out of the city. There was shelling and street-to-street fighting through April 25 and 26.

On April 26, the mujahedin leaders still in Pakistan announced a new power-sharing agreement, the Peshawar Accords. The agreement provided for Sibghatullah Mujaddidi, a relatively independent religious leader with a small political party, to become acting president of Afghanistan for two months, followed by Jamiat's political leader, Burhanuddin Rabbani, for another four months. After Rabbani's term, a shura was to choose an interim government to rule the country for eighteen more months, after

---

[20] Mohammad Nabi Azimi, *Ordu va Siyasat*, pp. 557-563. Azimi, who was a high level officer in the Afghan Army in this period, claims to have personally witnessed some of the discussions between Najibullah and Sevan preceding the fall of Kabul, and suggests that Najibullah did not discuss the idea of departing from Kabul with his closest Afghan advisors and staff.

which elections would be held. According to the agreement, Massoud was to act as Afghanistan's interim minister of defense. Hekmatyar was entirely sidelined from the government.

By April 27, Hekmatyar's main forces had been pushed to the south of Kabul, but remained within artillery range. The city was breached, however, and all the mujahedin parties, including Ittihad, Wahdat, and Harakat, now entered the city. Thousands of former government soldiers and police now switched their allegiances to the militias or to the Massoud-led forces in Mujaddidi's new government. Others just deserted. Some of the Pashtun officials who had earlier sided with Hezb-e Islami now left Kabul and allied with Hekmatyar to the south; some others joined the predominately Pashtun Ittihad party.[21] Kabul had suffered a few days of fighting, but was generally intact. The Soviet-backed government had fallen, with minimal damage to the city.

Jamiat commander Ahmed Shah Massoud on April 18, 1992, speaking to commanders on a field telephone just north of Kabul, soon after meeting with Junbish commander General Rashid Dostum. Jamiat and Junbish forces moved into Kabul six days later, while Hezb-e Islami forces entered the city from the south.
© 1992 Robert Nickelsberg

---

[21] For more information on ethnic identities and political alliances during this period, see Saikal, "The Rabbani Government, 1992-1996" in *Fundamentalism Reborn*, pp. 30-37, and Rubin, *The Search for Peace in Afghanistan*, pp. 128-129.

Defecting soldiers from the Soviet-backed government greet Jamiat mujahedin on the Jalalabad road, east of Kabul, April 25, 1992. After Najibullah's resignation, government forces put up no resistance to the mujahedin and Kabul was captured without fighting. The subsequent violence within the city was primarily due to rivalries among mujahedin factions. © 1992 Robert Nickelsberg

Junbish troops in a street battle with Hezb-e Islami forces in eastern Kabul, April 25, 1992.
© 1992 Robert Nickelsberg

HISTORICAL BACKGROUND

Junbish troops carrying rocket propelled grenades, south Kabul, April 25, 1992. © 1992 Robert Nickelsberg

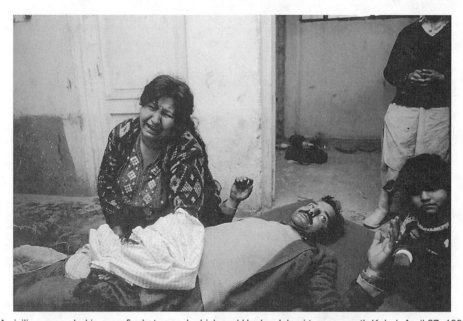

A civilian, wounded in crossfire between Junbish and Hezb-e Islami troops, south Kabul, April 27, 1992. © 1992 Robert Nickelsberg

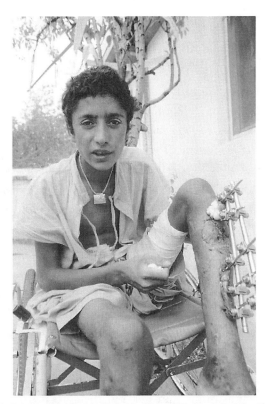

A boy wounded during street battles in Kabul in May 1992, treated at the Karte Seh hospital in west Kabul, May 1992. Tens of thousands of civilians were killed or injured in fighting in Kabul in 1992-1993. © 1992 Robert Nickelsberg

III. The Battle for Kabul: April 1992-March 1993

[Washington Post, May 3, 1992]   Kabul today is anything but a city basking in triumph. . . .   [R]ockets and shells continue to crash into residential neighborhoods, fired by the forces of fundamentalist guerrilla leader Gulbuddin Hekmatyar. . . . Hundreds of civilians lie in hospitals lacking electricity, water, and basic sterilization equipment.   More arrive each day. . . .   Heavily armed, ethnically divided guerrillas and militiamen prowl the city streets, defending patchwork blocks from their rivals, speaking in heated tones about their various enemies and sometimes looting homes and shops. . . .[22]

The small measure of calm restored after Hekmatyar's retreat to the south was not to last.   Many of the factions still in the city were openly hostile to one another, and Hekmatyar still wanted a major share of power in the new government.

After peace talks between Massoud and Hekmatyar on May 25, the government initially agreed to name Hekmatyar as prime minister, but the agreement collapsed in less than a week, when President Mujaddidi's plane came under rocket fire as he returned from a trip to Islamabad on May 29.   Mujaddidi claimed that both Hekmatyar's forces and former agents from the Najibullah government had conducted the attack, and that Hekmatyar had earlier threated to shoot down his plane.[23]   Meanwhile, Hekmatyar continued to demand that Dostum's Uzbek militias leave Kabul (which might then allow him to seize the city and expel Massoud's forces).[24]   By May 30, Jamiat and Junbish forces were again fighting with Hetmatyar's forces in the south of the city.   Hekmatyar began shelling and rocketing Kabul in early June, hitting all areas of the city, and Junbish and Jamiat forces shelled areas to the south of the city.   Meanwhile, Sunni Ittihad and Shi'a Wahdat factions in Kabul began fighting with one another in west Kabul.

---

[22] Steve Coll, "Afghanistan's Fate: Healing or Disintegration?" *Washington Post*, May 3, 1992.

[23] Sharon Herbaugh, "President Accuses Rebels, Communists Of Trying To Kill Him," Associated Press, May 31, 1992.   Herbaugh quoted Abdul Qadir Qaryab, a spokesman for Hezb-e Islami, dening the allegations: "If we had done it, we would have used at least 20 missiles and left no chance for survival, but we would never do that."

[24] For an overview of Hekmatyar's public statements during this period, see Sangar, *Neem Negahi Bar E'telafhay-e Tanzimi dar Afghanistan*, pp. 115-116, and sources cited therein.

As shown in sections below, the fighting between Jamiat and Hezb-e Islami, along with the clashes between Ittihad and Wahdat and later conflicts between Wahdat and Jamiat, led to tens of thousands civilian deaths and injuries, and caused hundreds of thousands to flee Kabul for safer areas.

A: April – December 1992

Ethnic fighting in West Kabul and the Hezb-e Islami attacks on Kabul

This section describes inter-factional hostilities in West Kabul and rocket and artillery attacks on Kabul by Hezb-e Islami forces to the south of the city. The section concludes with a section discussing the violations of international humanitarian law and human rights law which took place during these hostilities.

Wahdat, Ittihad and Jamiat in West Kabul

In May 1992, mere days after Hekmatyar was first driven from Kabul, the predominately Sunni-Pashtun Ittihad forces (under Abdul Rabb al-Rasul Sayyaf) and the predominately Shi'a-Hazara Wahdat forces (under Abdul Ali Mazari) began skirmishing in west Kabul, shooting rockets at each other and engaging in street battles. Each sought to dislodge the other from various neighborhoods or government buildings which each force occupied.

The battles, taking place in the midst of a dense civilian setting, predictably caused high numbers of casualties and lead to widespread destruction of civilian homes and infrastructure. The battles also became increasingly meaningless as the buildings each side occupied in the areas in dispute disintegrated into rubble. Much of west Kabul remains in ruins as of mid-2005, mostly because of fighting in 1992-1996.

There is no single explanation of which side started the fighting between Ittihad and Wahdat. Some observers believe the first problems arose over a relatively mundane issue: posters. Ittihad and Wahdat forces were reportedly tearing down posters of each other's leaders—Mazari and Sayyaf—which in turn led to arguments between the two side's troops, in turn leading to conflict between the forces.

A high-level Afghan military officer, General Mohammed Nabi Azimi, who served as a Soviet-era general and was cooperating at the time with the new government to create a national army, recounted in his 1998 memoirs the beginning of the fighting between Wahdat and Ittihad forces:

The first battle between Hazaras and Ittihad-e Islami began on 31 May 1992. First, four members of Hezb-e Wahdat's leadership were assassinated in the area near the Kabul Silo—Karimi, Sayyid Isma'il Hosseini, Chaman Ali Abuzar, and Vaseegh—of whom the first three were members of the central committee of the party. Shura-e Nazar [i.e., government officials] informed Hezb-e Wahdat that Sayyaf's men had assassinated them. Next, the car of Haji Shir Alam [a top Ittihad commander] was stopped by Hezb-e Wahdat near the Pol-e Sorkh area, and after releasing him, there was firing at the car which killed one of the passengers.[25]

Regardless of the proximate causes of the first clashes, the fact that conflict arose between Ittihad and Wahdat forces was not suprising. There was high tension between Wahdat, who were predominately Shi'a Muslims, and the Sunni Ittihad faction, whose members follow an ultra-conservative Islamic creed, Wahabbism, which views Shi'ism as heretical. A great deal of tension was also caused by the influence of foreign combatants and foreign military advisors and intelligence agents from Iran and possibly Saudi Arabia, who were working with some of the factions—Iranians with Wahdat and Saudis with Ittihad. Numerous Iranian agents were assisting Wahdat forces, as Iran was attempting to maximize Wahdat's military power and influence in the new government. Saudi agents of some sort, private or governmental, were trying to strengthen Sayyaf and his Ittihad faction to the same end.

Rare ceasefires, usually negotiated by Jamiat commanders, representatives of Mujaddidi or Rabbani, or officials from the International Committee of the Red Cross (ICRC), commonly collapsed within days. Compounding the problem, some of the other parties in Kabul periodically joined the fighting at various times, serving to intensify the conflict. Harakat forces sometimes joined the fight with Wahdat against Ittihad. After Wahdat attacked Jamiat positions in July 1992, and hit civilian areas around them, Massoud's troops launched retaliatory artillery attacks on west Kabul (which likewise killed numerous civilians).[26]

Human Rights Watch interviewed scores of witnesses and victims of the fighting in west Kabul in 1992 who described the violence and its effect on the civilian population.

---

[25] Mohammed Nabi Azimi, *Ordu va Siyasat*, p. 606 [translation by Human Rights Watch].

[26] See John Jennings, "Warring rebel groups blast Afghan capital," Associated Press, July 19, 1992; Suzy Price, "Kabul shelling injures hundreds of people," Reuters, July 19, 1992.

S.K., a health worker in a hospital in west Kabul, described the horror of everyday life after fighting started in Kohte-e Sangi, a neighborhood in the west:

> What can I say? What I saw in those days I can never forget. Hundreds of people were wounded when they fought—every time they fought. The hospital would be full of patients, overwhelmed; we couldn't treat everyone who was brought there. People were dying in the halls. People would not get treatment. There were dead bodies everywhere, and blood. When the fighting was very bad, and we couldn't transport anyone anywhere, there would be dead bodies in the hospital for weeks at a time. . . . Whenever the journalists came, they would ask the same questions: "How many rockets hit? How many were killed? How many were injured?" That's all they were interested in. . . .
>
> I saw dead bodies in the streets, and everywhere, all around west Kabul. In the hospital there were so many dead bodies, and because of the fighting, people could not come to take away the bodies.[27]

S.K. said that hospitals in west Kabul were repeatedly hit during the fighting between Ittihad/Jamiat and Wahdat. "One time, the children's ward at the hospital was hit, and twice the operating theatre. Patients were killed, and staff."[28]

A Kabul resident told Human Rights Watch about terrible scenes he encountered in west Kabul early in the summer of 1992:

> My wife was delivering our first child. Because I was poor, we were in our home, we could not leave to go anywhere [i.e. to a hospital]. So my wife told me to bring her sister, to help. So I went to west Kabul, to Qargha [on the border of Paghman district], to get her. . . . [T]he fighting had started while I was there. So we took the road up through Afshar. So we were going on the road, my sister-in-law on the bicycle behind me.

---

[27] Human Rights Watch interview with S.K., Afghan medical worker in Karte Seh (West Kabul) during early 1990's, Kabul, July 9, 2003.

[28] Ibid.

From Qargha to Afshar, on the road, I saw many corpses—seventeen, eighteen, I don't know—all civilians. They were commuters, people riding on the road [i.e., on bicycles], not fighters. Their bodies were swollen up. Also, I saw combatants, Hazaras, tied to trees, shot dead. I saw four fighters like this. My sister-in-law, of course, was very upset, and she started vomiting, so I had to stop. She was vomiting, and could not go on. Till this day, she does not eat meat. . . . So we turned back. We went back to Qargha, and then we went on another road. . . . When I got to my home, my wife had delivered my first child, and my first child was dead. To bury him was very difficult, with so much fighting going on, it was very difficult.[29]

An Afghan journalist who worked regularly in west Kabul through 1992 described how the fighting typically took place:

They were constantly shelling the civilian areas of west Kabul, and Afshar. . . . Shura-e Nazar would sometimes attack them from the zoo, and the silo [a grain warehouse in west Kabul]. Sayyaf's forces would attack from the west: Dasht-e Barchi [to the southwest] and Kohte-e Sangi [central west Kabul]. West Kabul was destroyed by the fighting between Ittihad and Wahdat, and by the artillery and rockets fired by Shura-e Nazar off of Television Mountain and Mamorine [the two peaks in the center of Kabul city]. . . . I went to a lot of places where the rockets and shells would fall. I saw many bodies, terrible sights. [30]

The first week of June 1992 was particularly bad, as Hekmatyar's forces were also launching artillery attacks on the city from the south.[31] (For more on Hekmatyar's shelling of the city, see the following section). Jamilurrahman Kamgar, a resident of Kabul who later published his contemporaneous chronicle of events in this period, wrote of heavy clashes between Wahdat and Ittihad forces, including attacks on a government mediator attempting to stop the fighting (June 2); the abduction of dozens of civilians by Hazara and Ittihad forces (June 3); hundreds of injuries and deaths, the

---

[29] Human Rights Watch interview with F.R.G., Kabul resident, Kabul, July 3, 2003.

[30] Human Rights Watch interview with O.U., Afghan journalist, Kabul, July 13, 2003.

[31] Health officials in Kabul told Agence France-Presse on June 9, 1992 that 100 people were killed and 400 wounded during the first week of June. Agence France-Presse news dispatch, June 9, 1992.

Red Cross hospital filled to capacity, and hundreds of families forced to leave destroyed houses (June 5).[32]

Sharon Herbaugh, a correspondent with Associated Press who died in a helicopter crash north of Kabul in 1993, filed a dispatch on June 5:

> [Friday, June 5, 1992] -- [A]ttacks continued, and more shops, schools and homes were destroyed in the ravaged capital. At least 20 more people were killed and 100 others injured. . . . Rival forces pounded each other with rockets and mortars, destroying entire blocks of shops and houses, and knocking down power lines. In downtown Kabul, rockets slammed into three empty schools, killing four passers-by and setting fires. Missiles also fell on a house in northern Kabul, killing a family of six, witnesses said. Unidentified gunmen raked a row of shops near the Kabul zoo, killing or injuring 10 people, witnesses said. . . . Residents in predominantly Shiite neighborhoods also accused Sunni rebels of looting shops and houses, killing prisoners, gouging out the eyes of wounded guerrillas and burning dead bodies.[33]

A journalist from Agence France-Presse saw hundreds of civilians fleeing from the west the same week, and witnessed some being shot by random gunfire and wounded children being carted to hospitals in wheelbarrows.[34]

One civilian who lived near the large grain silo in west Kabul described fighting between Wahdat and Ittihad that he believes took place in June 1992, right after a brief ceasefire:

---

[32] Jamilurrahman Kamgar, *Havadess-e Tarikhi-e Afghanistan 1990-1997 ("Afghanistan's Historic Events")* (Peshawar: Markaz-e Nashrati Meyvand, 2000), pp. 66-68 [translation by Human Rights Watch]. Kamgar also wrote of nighttime artillery barrages on Hezb-e Islami positions, by Junbish militias loyal to General Rashid Dostum, "whose flares turned the night into day" (June 10).

[33] Sharon Herbaugh, "Pro-Government militias intervene as fighting continues in Kabul," Associated Press, June 5, 1992. See also Andrew Roche, "Gunbattles rage in Kabul, death toll over 100," Reuters, June 5, 1992: "At least three civilians were shot dead on Friday morning [June 5], witnesses said. Residents scurried out of the area and units from neutral guerrilla factions sealed off road junctions around the maze of alleys near Temur Shahi Park as bullets flew over rooftops. . . ."

[34] Agence France-Presse dispatch, June 2, 1992.

People were really hoping [the ceasefire] would last: they were moving about, doing things that they hadn't been able to do until then. . . . It was around nine o' clock in the morning.

Suddenly, there was an explosion and a lot of firing of weapons. Everything was bullets, it was very severe. Everyone was rushing to flee from the violence. Husbands forgot wives, brothers forgot sisters, mothers forgot children, uncles forgot nephews—everyone was running away, and could only think of safety. . . . People were fleeing into our neighborhood because it was controlled by Shura-e Nazar. Wahdat was attacking from the south side of Kohte-e Sangi [a traffic roundabout south of the silo], and Sayyaf's forces were in Khushal Khan [to the west of the silo]. Both sides wanted to seize the property in that area: they wanted to use the places there to establish military positions. Both sides marched into the civilian areas and took up positions in people's houses. They were shooting at each other with rockets, guns, all sorts of weapons.

My house was where Shura-e Nazar had a checkpoint. I could see the women and men rushing away from the fighting, running down the street towards us. At the same time, some of the bullets, or shrapnel from the explosions, was hitting people. So men and women were falling down into the street. They would be running, and then the bullets would hit them, and they would fall down. The other people just kept running, and were not bothering to save those who fell. They were all rushing to save themselves. It was a terrible day. . . .

They were shooting everywhere. Everything was being hit: civilians, anything. Sayyaf's forces were shooting off their guns and rockets, they were flying into the side of Mamorine mountain [behind the silo], where there are houses and where the civilians were fleeing to, behind the silo. Rockets were going everywhere. The fighting lasted until dark. Sayyaf's troops came up into our neighborhood. We could see the Kandahari people [Pashtuns from Kandahar city] among Sayyaf's troops.[35]

A journalist in Kabul documented severe attacks on Hazara households by Ittihad troops on the night of June 4, 1992, interviewing residents who reported that Ittihad

---

[35] Human Rights Watch interview with F.K.Z., resident of west Kabul, Kabul, July 9, 2003.

troops had attacked and looted homes in Kohte-e Sangi, and killed six civilians. "The guerrillas were going from house to house, saying they wanted to kill all the Shi'as," one frightened resident told the journalist.[36]

Fighting continued through the month and into the summer. Jamhuriat hospital, near the Interior Ministry, had all its windows blown out and closed around June 24. Journalists who visited the hospital later in the week saw "a scene of utter despair"—no doctors or nurses, surgery patients lying in their own excrement and urine.[37]

Rocketing and shelling by Hezb-e Islami

West Kabul was not the only danger zone in the city. As Ittihad and Wahdat fought in the west, with occasional flare-ups involving Jamiat, Hekmatyar's Hezb-e Islami forces to the south continued to launch attacks on the city with rockets and artillery—attacks which were often aimed at the city as a whole, and not directed at specific military targets. Cumulatively, these were the most deadly attacks of the period.

President Mujaddidi handed over formal power to Rabbani at the end of June—as provided for in the Peshawar Accords—although Rabbani and Massoud's forces already controlled most security apparatuses and ministries in the capital. Hekmatyar continued to refuse to join the government. Hekmatyar's Hezb-e Islami forces increased their rocket and shell attacks on the city. Shells and rockets fell everywhere.

Conditions were such that anyone in Kabul could be killed at any time, almost anywhere: rockets and shells would hit homes, offices, bus stations, schools, or markets.[38] Kabul residents were often able to tell Human Rights Watch about rocket and artillery attacks

---

[36] Andrew Roche, "Gunbattles rage in Kabul, death toll over 100," Reuters, June 5, 1992.

[37] Kurt Schork, "Fighting Erupts in Center of Kabul," Reuters, June 25, 1992; and "Kabul—'Beirut without the Green Line,'" Reuters, June 26, 1992.

[38] Numerous media stories over the summer of 1992 documented the day-to-day violence. Archive footage of the British Broadcasting Corporation from April through August show artillery and rocket explosions in various parts of Kabul, and scenes of wounded and dead from Kabul's hospitals. Print journalists wrote extensively about the carnage through the year. See, e.g., John Pomfret, "Rocket Attack Terrorizes Musicians' Neighborhood," Associated Press, May 5, 1992; Sharon Herbaugh, "Rebel Faction Hammers Afghan Capital," Associated Press, May 5, 1992; "Fighting follows attempt on Afghan leader's life," Associated Press, May 31, 1992; Kurt Schork, "Afghan Factions Battle on Edge of Kabul," Reuters, June 24, 1992; "At least 48 killed in Kabul by rocket barrage," Reuters, July 4, 1992; "At least 100 dead in heavy fighting in Kabul," Agence France-Presse, July 5, 1992; "Rebel rocket attacks kill at least 50," Associated Press, July 5, 1992; "Rebels Rocket Kabul," Associated Press, August 6, 1992; John Jennings, "Rival Factions Shell Afghan Capital," August 8, 1992.

they say they knew were launched by Hekmatyar's forces, since they could often see rockets streaking in from the southwest, from areas under Hezb-e Islami control, or hear artillery being fired from the same area.

President Sibghatullah Mujaddidi's damaged airplane sitting on the tarmac at Kabul airport, May 29, 1992. The airplane, which had ferried Mujaddidi back from Islamabad, came under rocket attack while approaching Kabul airport. During the attack, the airplane's nosecone was sheared off and the co-pilot suffered shrapnel wounds, but the pilot managed to land safely. Mujaddidi, who was unharmed, blamed the attack on both Hekmatyar and agents of the former communist government. Jamiat and Junbish forces attacked Hekmatyar's Hezb-e Islami forces in the south of Kabul the next day. © 1992 Ed Grazda

One resident described to Human Rights Watch a rocket attack in the summer of 1992:

> Hekmatyar would rocket civilian areas all the time. One time, in the summer of 1992, I was standing behind the ministry of education, in Da Afghan Nan. I was waiting for a bus. A poor old man had a little cart and was selling chocolate and peanuts and almonds. The bus came, and it moved past me, so I moved down the block to get on the bus. I was getting on the bus, and suddenly, a rocket hit, where I had been. That man disappeared completely. No one found even one piece of his flesh. He completely disappeared. I think that 20 other people died there, and many more were wounded.[39]

---

[39] Human Rights Watch interview with A.S.F., Kabul resident, Kabul, July 2, 2003.

A woman in west Kabul described indiscriminate shelling in the west of Kabul in June 1992. She believes the attacks were by Hekmatyar's forces south of Kabul, since she heard artillery firing to the south during the attack:

> It was about 4 p.m., and I was baking some bread outside, over a fire. Suddenly, there was a big explosion. I took cover, on the ground. Then, there was another explosion. I got up and I could see this woman here [pointing to a neighbor who is crying], and she was just running about. [The women asked her neighbor to tell her story for her, and nodded throughout.] Her son had been sitting near this wall outside, where the artillery landed, and he was completely blown up. This woman here was running about, collecting pieces of [his] flesh in her apron, and crying. Her son's name was Sakhi. He was completely blown up, disappeared. Her grandson, Mukhtar, was also killed in the same explosion.[40]

A middle-aged man described a rocket attack that occurred around the same time, when Hekmatyar was firing rockets and artillery regularly into the city:

> We were in Micrayon 3 [in the east of the city, controlled by Jamiat and Junbish forces], it was about three o' clock in the afternoon. I was near this man's house, Alaz. We were in his yard, by a tree. He had some tomato plants, there were some good tomatoes, and I was asking him how much they cost. Suddenly there was a missile, and it hit the land, about 40 meters away. I dove to the ground. After a minute, I saw Alaz. He was bleeding. He was still alive. I asked him, I said, "Let's go to the hospital!" But he said: "No, there's no time. I am about to die." I held him, and then I carried him—he was bleeding from the side, the left side. My clothes were soaked with blood. The family came and gathered, they were screaming and crying. After about ten minutes, he died. This was in Block 19, in Micrayon.[41]

A journalist working in Kabul recounted seeing the terrible effects of the attacks in Kabul hospitals at the time, hospitals filled after the city came under fire from the south:

---

[40] Human Rights Watch interview with F.W., woman in Afshar, Kabul, July 2, 2003.

[41] Human Rights Watch interview with G.M.A., Kabul resident, December 7, 2003.

I remember pretty terrible scenes from those days, from the hospital. I saw children, kids, women wounded. Kids with their legs blown off. I once saw some kids arriving at the hospital in a car; their legs had been blown off by a bomb and they were just lying in the boot of the car. They were shelling into the city. It was Hekmatyar's forces.[42]

Two young men in Kabul hold up posters of Gulbuddin Hekmatyar, the military and political leader of Hezb-e Islami. © 1992 Ed Grazda

A photojournalist described the typical scene at a hospital in west Kabul after rocket attacks: "There'd be four or five bodies by the door, some coffins, then the bodies inside. . . . It was a grim scene, bleak. These rockets would rip pieces out of you."[43]

In August 1992, Hekmatyar's forces—who had already been rocketing civilian areas regularly since April—launched a new artillery and rocket blitz, bombarding all areas in Kabul held by Jamiat, Junbish, Ittihad, Harakat, and Wahdat—essentially the whole city. The apparent aim of the blitz was to force the government into a political compromise with Hezb-e Islami, as Hekmatyar likely did not have enough troops to launch an actual invasion of the city.

During the attack, hundreds of homes were destroyed, approximately 1,800 to 2,500 persons were killed, and thousands more were injured.[44] Governmental functions,

---

[42] Human Rights Watch telephone interview with Jeremy Bowen, correspondent with the British Broadcasting Corporation in Kabul in 1992, April 12, 2004.

[43] Human Rights Watch interview with R.N., photojournalist, New York, December 18, 2004.

already severely hampered, ceased. The Presidential Palace and numerous government buildings were hit, as well as the headquarters of the Red Cross and at least two of its hospitals. The city's water and electricity grids were severely damaged.[45] On some days, shells and rockets fell without interruption, and the city was gripped with terror.

The contemporaneous notes of a Kabul resident, Jamilurrahman Kamgar, who was quoted above, chronicle the daily barrage:

> August 1, 1992: Kabul's airport came under rocket attack. Hezb-e Islami took responsibility and said [via the radio]: these attacks were a response to the government's attacks on southern Kabul yesterday.

> August 2, 1992: Nearly 150 rockets hit different parts of Kabul; the government blamed Hekmatyar. . . . As a result of the attacks, many people were killed.

> August 5, 1992: The recent missile attacks have killed 50 people and injured nearly 150.

> August 10, 1992: At 5 a.m. there was heavy fighting between government forces and Hezb-e Islami. The government said that Hezb forces attacked from three directions, Chelsatoon, Darulaman and Maranjan mountain. There was not enough medicine in the hospitals

---

[44] Interim Report on the Situation of Human Rights in Afghanistan, prepared by Felix Ermacora, Special Rapporteur on Afghanistan for the U.N. Commission on Human Rights, November 17, 1992, U.N. Doc A/47/656, para. 34 (citing reports of 1,800 killed, thousands wounded); Human Rights Watch interviews with former U.N. officials working in Afghanistan in 1992, Kabul, December 10 and 11, 2003.

[45] For detailed accounts of the August 1992 attacks on Kabul, see Interim Report of the Special Rapporteur, November 17, 1992, para. 34; Barnett R. Rubin, *The Fragmentation of Afghanistan*, pp. 272-273 (citing U.N. Department of Humanitarian Affairs, "Note on Winter Emergency Needs in Afghanistan," November 1, 1992, and U.N. Office for the Co-ordination of Humanitarian and Economic Assistance Programmes Relating to Afghanistan, "Immediate Humanitarian Needs in Afghanistan Resulting from the Current Hostilities," press release, August 23, 1992); Saikal, "The Rabbani Government, 1992-1996" in *Fundamentalism Reborn*, p 33; Goodson, *Afghanistan's Endless War*, pp. 74-75. See also, John Jennings, "Rival factions shell Afghan capital," Associated Press, August 8, 1992; "Residents curse rebel rivalries," Associated Press, August 15, 1992; Mushahid Hussain, "Kabul and rebels claim advances," Inter Press Service Global Information Network, August 21, 1992.

and medical personnel could not be seen. A shell struck the Red Cross
hospital.

August 11, 1992: Nearly a thousand rockets hit various parts of the city
of Kabul. The airport sustained at least 250 hits. It's possible that a
thousand people were killed. These attacks came from Hekmatyar's
direction. . . .

August 14, 1992: The war is progressing severely. The people of Kabul
are escaping. The Pol-e Charkhi prison has become a refuge. . . .[46]

Ittihad and Jamiat forces, in turn, were launching artillery and rocket attacks on
Hekmatyar's positions to the south, which were also hitting civilian areas in the
southwest of Kabul.

Hamid Karzai, now the president of Afghanistan and at the time a deputy foreign
minister in the government, told a journalist in Kabul on August 9, 1992: "I don't know
what's going to happen. . . . We're just killing each other. It's senseless."[47]

President Sibghatullah Mujaddidi speaking at a news conference in June 1992. Hamid Karzai, deputy foreign
minister at the time, is visible just beyond the microphone. © 1992 Ed Grazda

---

[46] Kamgar, *Havadess-e Tarikhi*, pp. 78-80 [translation by Human Rights Watch].

[47] "Fighting in Afghanistan's Capital Kills 35," Associated Press, August 9, 1992.

Kabul's hospitals were hard pressed to keep up with the violence. An ICRC representative in Kabul, quoted in a U.N. memorandum in 1992, described the situation on August 13, 1992 in the following terms:

> This afternoon we had 353 patients in our hospital which has only 300 beds. There are patients in the entrance hall, in the courtyard. Thirty-eight wounded died before they could be treated, 77 were waiting to be operated on, 60 were admitted this afternoon, 91 yesterday and 183 Saturday.[48]

The chief of the United Nations mission in Kabul told journalists on August 20:

> It's a terrible situation. The government no longer controls anything; there is no longer law and order. The streets are entirely deserted, except for armed soldiers. Water and electric power have been cut off for nearly a week and my colleagues from WHO [the World Health Organization] are afraid of an outbreak of epidemics.[49]

The United Nations estimated that approximately 500,000 persons fled Kabul by the end of the summer for safer areas inside and outside of Afghanistan, primarily because of Hekmatyar's rocket and artillery attacks.[50]

Violations of International Humanitarian Law

The armed conflict in Afghanistan in 1992-93 was a non-international (internal) armed conflict in which the Geneva Conventions and customary international humanitarian law applied to government forces and non-state armed groups. (The specific legal status of the conflict and culpability of specific individuals are discussed in more detail in section IV below.)

Many of the events described above amounted to war crimes. Launching indiscriminate attacks that may be expected to cause loss of civilian life, or intentionally targeting the civilian population and civilian objects, are violations of international humanitarian law, amounting to war crimes. More specifically, customary international law prohibits

---

[48] Interim Report of the Special Rapporteur, November 17, 1992, para. 35.

[49] Philip Bruno, "La seconde bataille de Kaboul 'Le gouvernement ne contrôle plus rien,'" Le Monde, August 20, 1992.

[50] See Rubin, *The Fragmentation of Afghanistan*, pp. 272-273 (citing U.N. documents).

treating an entire city as a single military objective,[51] and requires belligerents to take feasible precautions to protect civilians against the effects of attacks, including choosing methods and means of warfare that avoid loss of civilian life, and to cancel or suspend attacks causing unnecessary civilian loss. In addition, deliberate and widespread killing of civilians, through prolonged indiscriminate shelling and artillery attacks, can amount to crimes against humanity.[52]

Individuals—combatants and civilians—are criminally responsible for war crimes they commit. Commanders are criminally liable for war crimes committed pursuant to their orders or as a matter of command responsibility. Command responsibility makes a commander culpable for war crimes committed by subordinates if the commander knew or had reason to know such crimes were being committed and did not take all necessary and reasonable measures to prevent the crimes, or punish those responsible for crimes already committed.[53]

With respect to **Wahdat, Ittihad, and Jamiat** hostilities in west Kabul, there is compelling evidence that factions regularly and intentionally targeted civilians and civilian areas for attack, and recklesslessly and indiscriminately fired weapons into civilian areas. There is little evidence that the factions made meaningful efforts during hostilities to avoid harming civilians or stopped attacks once the harm to civilians was evident.

One Afghan journalist, quoted above, told Human Rights Watch that he witnessed on several occasions Ittihad and Wahdat forces intentionally firing rockets into occupied civilian homes during hostilities in 1992.[54] He also said that Jamiat forces, once they joined Ittihad in battling Wahdat late in 1992, regularly fired randomly into civilian areas in west Kabul:

> It was a normal, everyday experience that they would fire off of the television mountain, and from the top of Karte Mamorine, at Dasht-e

---

[51] See Section IV below. Provisions of Article 51 of the Geneva Conventions Additional Protocol I, which are considered generally to amount to customary international law for international or non-international conflicts, prohibit indiscriminate attacks "by bombardment" which treat "as a single military objective a number of clearly separated and distinct military objectives located in a city. . . ." Protocol I (1977) Additional to the Geneva Conventions of 1949 ("Protocol I"), art. 51 (5).

[52] For more on the definition of crimes against humanity, see section IV below.

[53] See section IV below.

[54] Human Rights Watch interview with O.U., Afghan journalist, Kabul, July 13, 2003.

Barchi, Karte Seh [District 3], and Deh Mazang. Also, on Koiatub [or Koiatab] mountain, there was a tank on top of it. This was the place that during the King's time [before 1973] they would fire off a canon there, everyday at 12 noon. They would fire from there also.[55]

A former high-level official in Shura-e Nazar confirmed that Jamiat troops on the Mamorine mountain (the western peak next to Television Mountain and above west Kabul) regularly launched rockets and artillery into the civilian areas of west Kabul in 1992 and 1993.[56]

"There was little effort [by any of the factions] to aim at targets," an international journalist told Human Rights Watch, describing the fighting between Wahdat, Ittihad, and Jamiat.[57] "It was Massoud and Sayyaf versus the Hazaras. Deh Mazang [an area in west Kabul] was a front line. They would shoot at anything in between, whatever it was."[58]

S.K., a hospital worker quoted above, also told Human Rights Watch about the attacks on civilians by Jamiat forces stationed on Television Mountain in the center of Kabul:

> There was a time when the Jamiat troops on TV Mountain would target anything on Alaudin Street [the main road running north-south through Karte Seh]. They would target anything that moved, even a cat. . . .
>
> I remember [one time] I went out to go to this clinic [to obtain medical equipment], and as soon as they saw me on that mountain they were shooting.
>
> Anything that looked like a human being would be targeted. They shot everything: rockets, shells, bullets. There were times when the streets were littered with bullets. . . .[59]

---

[55] Ibid.

[56] Human Rights Watch interview with S.A.R., former Shura-e Nazar official, Kabul, July 20, 2003.

[57] Human Rights Watch interview with Suzy Price, correspondent for the British Broadcasting Corporation and Reuters, New York, April 1, 2004.

[58] Ibid.

[59] Human Rights Watch interview with S.K., Afghan medical worker in Karte Seh (West Kabul) during early 1990's, Kabul, July 9, 2003.

A photojournalist who worked in Kabul regularly during 1992, and visited numerous military posts, told Human Rights Watch about Jamiat forces firing into civilian areas from the same mountain:

> Yeah, they'd fire off T.V. Mountain all the time. Some of the wackos up there, they'd get bored. They'd strafe the neighborhoods below with anti-aircraft fire. For fun—just for the hell of it. The civilian homes below, near the zoo, by the traffic check-post, near the silo. They wouldn't aim at any ministries [government buildings], that'd be their own turf. No, they'd fire toward the southwest, and not just at Wahdat but at civilians. And there were Tajiks down there too [same ethnicity as Jamiat], not just Shi'as [Hazaras are predominately Shi'a].[60]

Wahdat, Ittihad, and Jamiat forces regularly used imprecise weapons systems, including Sakr rockets and UB-16 and UB-32 S-5 airborne rocket launchers clumsily refitted onto tank turrets. The aiming of these rocket systems are considered "dumb" or non-precision.[61] Sakr rockets are "like bottle rockets," according to one military analyst,[62] and rocket systems generally as not designed for accuracy in close combat: they cannot be adequately aimed within urban settings or made to distinguish between military targets and civilian objects. The use of the makeshift S-5 system in particular, within Kabul city, demonstrated an utter disregard of the duty to use methods and means of attack that distinguish between civilian objects and military targets.[63]

Further research is needed into the exact command structure of the Wahdat, Ittihad, and Jamiat forces involved in the fighting detailed above. Discussion of the command

---

[60] Human Rights Watch interview with R.N., photojournalist, New York, December 18, 2004.

[61] Human Rights Watch telephone interview with Colonel Ron Bailey, weapons system expect, United States Marine Corps, December 20, 2004. Human Rights Watch interview with A.G., military analyst, New York, April 9, 2004.

[62] Human Rights Watch interview with A.G., military analyst, New York, April 9, 2004.

[63] A weapons expert who inspected photographs of Jamiat weapons systems in 1992 told Human Rights Watch that the UB airborne rocket launchers were essentially reckless: "[T]hey took them off a Hind [Soviet attack helicopter], and then attached them to the turret of the tank. But here's the thing: there's no accuracy at all with a system like that. There's no aiming. You can move the turret around, and you can raise the vehicles angle of elevation up and down, but there's no system to aim, and there's no mechanism to sight the system. It's just like they fire the mortars. You can aim it in the general direction of where you're shooting, but that's all." Human Rights Watch telephone interview with Colonel Ron Bailey, weapons system expert, United States Marine Corps, December 20, 2004.

structure of the Wahdat, Ittihad, and Jamiat forces, and the responsibility of individual commanders, appears in sections below and in Section IV.

Hezb-e Islami forces used artillery and rockets in a manner indicating that they were intentionally targeting civilian areas, failing to properly aim (with respect to artillery guns), recklessly using weapons which could not be aimed in a dense civilian setting (with respect to rockets), and treating the whole city as one unified military target.

With respect to artillery attacks, there is evidence that Hezb-e Islami had the capacity to aim artillery at military targets, but either recklessly chose not to do so, or intentionally aimed artillery at civilian objects instead, in violation of international humanitarian law. As the primary recipient of international assistance and training from Pakistan, the United States, and the United Kingdom, Hezb-e Islami was arguably the most well-trained mujahedin group in Kabul at the time. Many commanders and troops were trained by Pakistani, American, and British experts on the use of rocket and artillery systems. Journalists who visited sites held by Hezb-e Islami forces to the south of Kabul saw numerous D-30 122mm cannons that were being used for attacking Kabul—a relatively precise artillery system.[64] Reporting and footage from 1992 and 1993 suggests that Hezb-e Islami forces could, when they wanted to, precisely aim such artillery: BBC film footage from May 1992 shows accurate targeting of artillery by Hezb-e Islami of Jamiat and Junbish positions in Kabul.[65] Terence White, a correspondent with Agence France-Presse, reported precise artillery fire against Jamiat positions in south Kabul in early 1993.[66] Yet in many cases, including ones documented in this report, Hezb-e Islami artillery and rockets hit civilian areas, suggesting that they were either purposely targeting such areas, or recklessly aiming at Kabul as a whole. The prolonged timeframe in which the attacks took place, their scope, and their continued inaccuracy, strongly suggest there was neither a fixable problem with artillery aim calibration, nor weapons systems' failure. Accurate and aimable weapons were being shot into civilian areas in violation of international humanitarian law.

---

[64] Human Rights Watch telephone interview with John Jennings, April 10, 2004; Human Rights Watch telephone interview with Anthony Davis, July 9, 2004.

[65] This information is based on viewing by Human Rights Watch of stock film footage from April and May of 1992, on file with the libraries of the British Broadcasting Corporation.

[66] Terence White, "South Kabul under intense rebel bombardment, many casualties," Agence France-Presse, January 21, 1993 (Chelsitoon palace gardens in south Kabul, "once likened to a Greek temple setting, were being chewed up by the very accurate Hezb artillery barrage").

Hekmatyar's forces also often used BM-40, BM-22, BM-12 rocket launchers and Sakr Soviet-made rockets in their attacks on Kabul.[67] As noted earlier, such rocket systems are generally considered "dumb" or non-precision: these weapons are not designed for accuracy in close combat and cannot be adequately aimed within urban settings or made to distinguish between military targets and civilian objects.[68] The very use of such rocket systems within Kabul may have been an indiscriminate method or means of warfare in violation of international humanitarian law.

The pattern and characteristics of the attacks also suggest that Hekmatyar and his commanders were attacking the whole city, or treating the city itself as a single target.[69]

General Mohammed Nabi Azimi's memoirs, discussing the July and August blitzes, reinforce the view that Hekmatyar's forces bombarded civilian areas intentionally:

> So once again, Hekmatyar's heavy weapons roared and rained fire on Kabul. The height of the fighting and clashes was in late July and early August 1992. As soon as it became light, Hekmatyar's rocket launchers and artillery would come to life. Hekmatyar now controlled the Takht-e Shahi heights which command Kabul [to the south]. There, the artillery teams had wireless communication sets. Hekmatyar's artillery teams were reinforced by trained officers. . . . Hekmatyar could now accurately fire on military targets. But he preferred to fire on the city and defenseless civilians in order to create tension and dissatisfaction among the people against Rabbani and Massoud.[70]

---

[67] Human Rights Watch telephone interview with John Jennings, April 10, 2004; Human Rights Watch telephone interview with Anthony Davis, July 9, 2004. The Afghan Justice Project (see footnote 75 and accompanying text) also interviewed witnesses who described Hekmatyar's weaponry to include BM-21 rocket launchers.

[68] Anthony Davis, who is a military analyst with *Jane's Defense Weekly*, confirmed Hekmatyar's use of Sakr rockets in Kabul in 1992 and 1993 and described their inaccuracy: "These are aerial weapons; not pinpoint weapons. They're quite unsophisticated weapons. You fire them and then they're off: very inaccurate." Human Rights Watch telephone interview with Anthony Davis, July 9, 2004.

[69] See text in Section IV below outlining prohibitions on indiscriminate attacks including attacks "by bombardment" which treat "as a single military objective a number of clearly separated and distinct military objectives located in a city. . . ." from Protocol I (1977) Additional to the Geneva Conventions of 1949 ("Protocol I"), art. 51 (5).

[70] Mohammed Nabi Azimi, *Ordu va Siyasat*, pp.626-627 [translation by Human Rights Watch].

"They weren't picking out military targets," one journalist who witnessed the repeated attacks in Kabul told Human Rights Watch. "Once the shelling started, artillery would fall everywhere, across the city. Across the city, you could hear the shells."[71]

> The pattern of casualties, and how so many civilians died, suggested that they were firing indiscriminately. . . . I suppose, yes, they hit some military targets, whatever that means, but mostly the bombs were just hitting various parts of the city, and it was mostly civilians who were getting hit, as you would see at the hospital.[72]

Marc Biot, a medical official at the Jamuhuriat hospital, told Human Rights Watch:

> It was like this: At any moment a missile could fall. . . . When you were outside, you never knew if a missile would fall on your head. They were shooting them blindly, anywhere: into roads, markets, houses. . . . The most awful thing was that any bomb could fall on any place at any time. There was a clear political will to shell the city, as a city—to shell the city as a civilian place. The shelling was ubiquitous, everywhere.[73]

One journalist cited above, who visited Hezb-e Islami positions to the south of Kabul, suggested to Human Rights Watch that artillery spotters must have been intentionally directing artillery at civilian areas:

> We talked to the officers pretty regularly—they had spotters, observers. They insisted they were hitting military targets. But they [the officers] knew what was going on. Both Massoud and Hekmatyar had a lot of artillerymen who were trained. They could aim. Elevation and windage [lateral and vertical movement] could be changed. But they [Hezb-e Islami forces] were aiming into the city. They had spotters in the city: Hezb-e Islami were able to infiltrate Kabul, it was easy. The aim was to terrorize the population.[74]

---

[71] Human Rights Watch telephone interview with Jeremy Bowen, correspondent with the British Broadcasting Corporation in Kabul in 1992, April 12, 2004.

[72] Ibid.

[73] Human Rights Watch telephone interview with Marc Biot, official at Jamhuriat hospital in Kabul in 1992-1993, July 10, 2004.

[74] Human Rights Watch telephone interview with John Jennings, Associated Press correspondent in Kabul 1992-1993, April 10, 2004.

The testimony above suggests that Hezb-e Islami and Hekmatyar were deliberately targeting the city of Kabul as a whole entity, to terrorize and kill civilians.

Further investigation will be needed to determine the role of specific commanders in the attacks. According to the Afghan Justice Project, an independent non-governmental group that has investigated military operations in Afghanistan from 1979 through 2001,[75] besides Hekmatyar the following commanders had operation control over the military posts firing artillery and rockets at Kabul during the period discussed in this report:

- Commander Toran Khalil, chief artillery officer in Hezb-e Islami who supervised shelling and rocketing operations during late 1992 into 1993, commander of a base at an oil depot at the south of Charasiab, south of Kabul.
- Toran Amanullah, commander of the Firqa Sama, stationed at the Rishkor military base, south of Kabul.
- Commander Zardad, commander of a military post at the Lycee Shorwaki.
- Engineer Zulmai, of the Lashkar Issar, commander of a post at the Kotal Hindki pass to the south of Chilsatoon, south of Kabul, near the Rishkor base.
- Nur Rahman Panshiri, commander of a post in the village of Shahak, to the southeast of Kabul, directly controlled by the Sama division.
- General Wali Shah, an officer in the Najibullah government who joined Hezb-e Islami in 1992, commander of a base at Sang-e Nevishta, Logar, south of Kabul.
- Shura Nizami (military council) commanders Faiz Mohammad, Kashmir Khan, and Sabawon.

The legal responsibility of these Hezb-e Islami commanders, as well as Hekmatyar himself, is discussed further in section IV below.

Abductions, "Disappearances," Torture, and Other Mistreatment of Detainees

> [Reuters, June 4, 1992] *Gunfire and explosions echoed across western Kabul. . . . Guerrillas of the Hezb-e-Wahdat Shi'a alliance fought gunbattles with Sunni Ittehad-i-Islami fighters close to Kabul university, a Shi'a base, for the third day running. . . . Guerrillas of the two groups rounded up hundreds of civilians at gunpoint on Tuesday and Wednesday and took them to makeshift detention centres after demanding to see identity papers, which state the bearer's ethnic group, at street*

---

[75] See Afghan Justice Project, "Addressing the Past: The Legacy of War Crimes and the Political Transition in Afghanistan," January 2005 ("AJP report"), pp. 23-24.

checkpoints. Shi'a guerrillas took away Sunni Muslim ethnic Pashtuns, while Ittehad guerrillas detained ethnic Hazaras, who are Shi'as. Witnesses said some people were beaten with sticks as they were led away. . . .[76]

In addition to the war violence, the fighting between Ittihad and Wahdat through 1992 was spawning another problem with especially terrible effects on civilians: ethnic abductions. Ittihad and Wahdat forces were increasingly abducting civilians and holding them for ransom or exchange—Ittihad holding Hazaras, and Wahdat holding Pashtuns, Tajiks, and other non-Hazaras. A journalist told Human Rights Watch:

> There was a lot of kidnapping in the west. The commanders under Sayyaf and the commanders under Hizb-e Wahdat would stop buses or cars, and look for Hazaras and Pashtuns. Sayyaf's men would look for Hazaras. Hizb-e Wahdat forces would look for Pashtuns.[77]

As shown below, the practice seems to have begun in May of 1992. Gen. Mohammed Nabi Azimi, the high-level military officer quoted earlier in this report, described how the two forces began erecting checkpoints and engaging in routine abductions:

> Hazaras abducted Pashtuns and Pashtuns abducted Hazaras wherever they saw each other. They pulled out the fingernails of prisoners, cut off hands, cut off legs, even hammered nails into prisoners' skulls. Humans were kept in [shipping] containers and containers were set on fire. . . . Cruelty, injustice, and inhumanity began, and became a chronic disease; humanity and honor were crucified.[78]

Many of the civilians abducted by the two sides during this time were never seen again. Some did manage to be released, however, usually after prisoner exchanges or personal interventions by government officials or religious or tribal leaders with connections to those detained.

Human Rights Watch spoke with several former detainees in Kabul in 2003—Hazaras, Pashtuns, and Tajiks—who described their experiences. Their stories follow:

---

[76] Andrew Roche, "Guerrillas clash in Kabul, some hostages freed," Reuters, June 4, 1992.

[77] Human Rights Watch interview with O.U., Afghan journalist, Kabul, July 13, 2003.

[78] Mohammed Nabi Azimi, *Ordu va Siyasat*, p. 609 [translation by Human Rights Watch].

Abdul Ali Mazari, the military and political leader of Hezb-e Wahdat in the early 1990s. Mazari's faction, as well as Abdul Rabb al-Rasul Sayyaf's Ittihad faction, committed war crimes and other atrocities in west Kabul in the early 1990s. © 1994 Robert Nickelsberg

Abductions by Wahdat

A young Tajik man from west Kabul, who said he was held by Wahdat forces in December 1992 after some streets fighting that occurred near the government silo, told Human Rights Watch about his abduction and detention by men he identified as members of Wahdat:[79]

> [M]y brother came and said he wanted us to leave the area with him. We were talking about this, sitting in our home, drinking tea, when some gunmen [Wahdat] came and knocked on the door.
>
> "Whose house is this?" a commander said. He was at the door. —"It is mine," I said. —"What is your name?" I said my name was [deleted]. —"Where are you from?" he asked. —"Kabul," I said. —"You're lying," he said. He pulled out a list, and found my name on the list: my parents and brothers names were on the list also, and next to my name it said we were from Shomali [a predominately Tajik area north of Kabul]. The commander said, "Are you from Shomali?" And I said yes, that I

---

[79] Human Rights Watch interview with F.K.Z., resident of west Kabul, Kabul, July 9, 2003.

was studying in Kabul and lived there. He said, "Let's go inside," and pushed me into my own house. As I came in, I told my brother [with my hands] to hide himself, but he didn't understand. So then the commander saw him also. . . . Before taking us away, they arrested a guy from Wardak next door. He was complaining a lot, so they blindfolded him. . . . They put us all in a vehicle, and when we got to Kohte-e Sangi they put blindfolds on us too. After that, we couldn't see and could not understand where they were taking us. . . .

When the vehicle stopped, the men assumed they were at Dasht-e Barchi, where Wahdat had a base, but the man later discovered he was at Onchi Baghbanan [to the north of Dasht-e Barchi, about 4 kilometers west of Karte Seh].

> We got out. They threw the three of us into a container . . . . Then, a commander with two bodyguards came, and he came into the container, and questioned us. "You both are some guys from Shomali and you are helping Massoud!" he said. —I said, "I am a medical student; neither I nor my brother are soldiers. We are from Shomali, but we are not soldiers." —"Keep quiet," he said. And then the guards cocked their Kalashnikovs [assault rifles]. The commander signaled to his troops to take us away. We were blindfolded, and made to walk somewhere else. They were kicking us. Finally, we were imprisoned in a small room.

The man said he and the other prisoners were later given a plate of rice to share. But that night, other prisoners were brought in and together they were transported to another site:

> We drove there. Then they threw us into a basement—no, the basement of a basement. It was dark, and dirty, and very cold. We could hear machine guns were being fired above us. We assumed that we were somewhere near the front line.

> That night, they brought three other guys: a guy from Jalalabad, a worker from Shomali, and a lecturer from the university. They were also thrown into the basement with us. There was not enough room for us. There was dirty air, and it was completely, completely dark. We were there for several days. They would let us out two times a day, to urinate.

The basement room was freezing, and the young man said at times he was so numb that he feared he was going to die. After a week, the man and his brother were released, apparently because of the intervention of relatives who were able to make contacts with Wahdat commanders. But the man said his fellow prisoners met a different fate:

> Those other people who we were imprisoned with were never released. They disappeared. I know because they told us to find their families. And I contacted their families, several times. Those families pressured us, to help them. We gave them some advice. But a month later those prisoners were not released. And later on, when I spoke with them again, I learned that those prisoners had never been released.

An elderly Pashtun man described being arrested by Wahdat forces in mid-May 1992, and seeing other prisoners killed by them:

> It was morning, I was going by Chelsatoon garden. I was with my 10-year-old son. We were stopped by Hezb-e Wahdat troops. Two men. They took us to Habibi high school. They didn't give me any problems at first, they were just questioning me. . . . But I saw this container nearby, with prisoners. The two men were arguing. One was saying, "Leave him, he's innocent." The other was saying, "No, we should arrest them because they're Pashtuns." They had arrested some other Pashtuns, and I saw them putting them into a container there.
>
> The first one was saying, "Put him in the container!" And the other was saying, "No, he has a young kid with him." Then the first one was saying, "No—he is Pashtun. Put him in the container!" Their argument lasted a few minutes. Finally, they let me go and I was set free.[80]

The man said the troops sometime soon after apparently fired a missile or rocket-propelled grenade into the container:

> I was walking away with my son. We heard the explosion. The container had been closed after they put the prisoners in it. I heard the explosion and I looked, and then I took my son and started to move away, because we were in danger. . . . When I looked I saw that all these people were running away from where the container was. . . . I heard

---

[80] Human Rights Watch interview with Y.N., Kabul, December 6, 2003.

screams from the container and there was smoke coming out of the hole. The rocket had penetrated and exploded. . . .[81]

Human Rights Watch interviewed several other Pashtuns and Tajiks held by Wahdat forces in 1992 and released when family members or acquaintances were able to convince leaders in the various factions to have them released. A senior civilian official in the Jamiat-dominated government told Human Rights Watch that numerous complaints were made to the government about Wahdat arrests, and that they documented that Wahdat had set up a prison at a compound in west Kabul called Qala Khana, run by a senior Wahdat commander called Shafi Diwana (Shafi the Mad), in which prisoners were tortured and killed.[82] Petitioners brought allegations to the Jamiat officials that Wahdat forces were burning the bodies of prisoners in brick-making furnaces in the compound.[83]

A health worker in west Kabul, quoted above, told Human Rights Watch that hospital staff in west Kabul knew that thousands of prisoners were kept by Wahdat forces in Dasht-e Barchi, and that they were sometimes able to negotiate to have them released, although most were never seen again.[84]

Abductions by Ittihad

As noted above, Ittihad was holding prisoners too. Human Rights Watch interviewed a Pashtun man who, despite his Pashtun ethnicity, was held by Ittihad forces in the summer of 1992 because of a non-ethnic dispute with troops. The man said he was put in detention with approximately thirty to forty Hazara prisoners who said they were abducted based on their ethnicity.[85] He described his experience:

> [S]ome of Sayyaf's men, from Paghman, came and took me. They were looking for my brother-in-law [because of a private financial dispute], but they took me instead, as a hostage. They took me to Khoshal Khan

---

[81] Ibid.

[82] Human Rights Watch interview with R.D., former official in the interim government 1992-1995, Kabul, July 16, 2003.

[83] Ibid.

[84] Human Rights Watch interview with S.K., Afghan medical worker in Karte Seh (West Kabul) during early 1990's, Kabul, July 9, 2003.

[85] The quotes and descriptions of this case are taken from a Human Rights Watch interview with F.R.G., Kabul resident, Kabul, July 3, 2003.

Mina, the headquarters for the electric buses, near the silos. They put me in a room there, and they told me that they would hold me there, for a night, and then I would be released. The commander there was named Tourgal. But the next day, Wahdat and Sayyaf started fighting.

That night, as fighting raged outside, the man said that the Ittihad forces brought in Hazara civilians: "Sayyaf's forces brought thirty or forty Hazara civilians. . . . They were not fighters, but civilians, old and young." Later in the night, according to the man, the Ittihad forces shot at the prisoners in their holding cell with an automatic weapon:

> [T]he fighting got severe. We could hear the artillery. There was a lot of shooting. I could hear these people, Sayyaf's people, talking about retreating. And at one point, one of them said to Commander Tourgal, "What should we do with these prisoners?" They were speaking in Pashto, and the Hazara people couldn't understand them. But I could understand. Somebody said, "Go and shoot them."

> I was near the door. When I heard this, I hurried away and hid away from the door, in the corner of the room [on the side of the room with the door]. A person came, and opened the door, and shot all over the room with his kalashnikov, on automatic. He just fired randomly all over the room. About ten people were killed, immediately, and four were wounded. . . . After, no one moved. We [who were still alive] were trembling with fear. The fighting outside was serious—the commander called on this guy to come back to fight at the windows with them, so the man left, to go back to fighting.

The prisoners were too afraid to move the dead bodies. But when the fighting stopped, the man desperately pleaded with the troops to release him: "The next time the troops came by, I rushed to the door and said, "Listen, I am a Pashtun, and I was not arrested with these people." The man said the troops then put him into another room, presumably because he was not Hazara. "I don't know what happened to the [other] people in that room," the man said.

Ultimately, the man was released after a relative, who knew some members of Ittihad, visited Sayyaf in Paghman, to plead for his release. The relative told Human Rights Watch that Sayyaf ordered another minister (the name is deleted here to protect the man and his relative) to order the man's release.[86] The minister then wrote an order to Commander Tourgal, the relative said, which he took to Tourgal, who then released the prisoner—a series of events that suggests that Sayyaf had knowledge of Ittihad's regular detention of civilians and that he had control over the commanders holding them.

Human Rights Watch interviewed numerous other Hazara men in west Kabul who were held by Ittihad forces in 1992 and early 1993, forced to work in manual labor for Ittihad forces (their stories are in the following section: "The Attack on Afshar").

Abuse of Prisoners

Human Rights Watch received consistent and credible testimony that many of the persons detained by Wahdat and Ittihad were forced to work, mistreated, or tortured while in the custody of Ittihad and Wahdat forces. S.K., a hospital worker quoted above, described seeing detainees after their release from both factions who were badly injured, who told her they had been subjected to torture and other mistreatment:

> I saw hostages who had been tortured: civilians and non-civilians. This was something common: people released by each side, their families would bring them to the hospital [because they had been abused in captivity]. Wahdat would capture Pashtuns and Tajiks, and Ittihad would capture Hazaras.

> I saw what they had done to them: People beaten up. People who had been tortured. They had put RPGs [Rocket Propelled Grenades] into the anus. They gang-raped girls. I saw these victims.[87]

Human Rights Watch interviewed several Afghan journalists who spoke with detainees in 1992 and 1993, who described abuses while in detention.[88] Journalists with the British Broadcasting Corporation and Associated Press in 1992 interviewed detainees of various ethnicities who related descriptions of their arrests and abuse.[89]

---

[86] Human Rights Watch interview with L.R.G., relative of the prisoner, Kabul, July 3, 2003.

[87] Human Rights Watch interview with S.K., Afghan medical worker, Kabul, July 9, 2003. See also testimony of H.K., Afghan NGO worker, below.

[88] Human Rights Watch interview with Y.U., Afghan journalist, Kabul, July 8, 2003; Human Rights Watch interview with O.U., Afghan journalist, Kabul, July 13, 2003.

[89] See e.g., Sharon Herbaugh, "Civilians Tell of Captivity, Torture by Rebels," Associated Press, June 6, 1992, quoting interview with released Hazara prisoner. "'We were kept in containers, so many of us that we couldn't sit down. They wouldn't give us food or water,' said Nadir Ali, a 22-year-old

It is likely that the abductions and abuse were fueled in part as retaliation for continuing atrocities. Abdul Haq, a mujahedin commander who served as police chief in Kabul in 1992 (Haq was later killed by Taliban forces in eastern Afghanistan in October 2001), told a journalist in 1992 that non-Wahdat and non-Ittihad commanders had worked to arrange large prisoner swaps between Wahdat and Ittihad in the first week of June, but that the exchanges collapsed after both sides saw that some prisoners had been tortured or mistreated.[90]

(Further descriptions of abuse of detainees captured by Ittihad and Wahdat appears in the "Rape" section below, and in the section "The Attack on Afshar" below.)

"Disappearances"

Human Rights Watch interviewed several families in west Kabul who said that their relatives had been abducted in 1992 by Wahdat or Ittihad, and never seen again. For fear of continuing threats to their security from the same factions, they refused to allow Human Rights Watch to use the names of their disappeared relatives.

In 1996, Afghan aid workers working in west Kabul published a book documenting some of the abductions and "disappearances" of persons from west Kabul, with names and pictures (when available) of victims.[91] The project, based on research conducted in 1993-1995, focused predominately on Hazara disappearances at the hands of Ittihad. But the book does detail abductions by Wahdat and Jamiat as well, and partly reveals the scope of the overall problem.

The book documents 671 cases of abductions and disappearances, mostly in west Kabul and mostly in 1992-1993. H.K.,[92] one of the books' researchers, told Human Rights Watch that over 1,000 people were reported missing in west Kabul in the first year after the fall of the Najibullah government:

Hazara candymaker who was held with [. . .] others at an abandoned interrogation center of the former secret police. He was clutching his right arm, which was swollen and probably broken from the blows with rifle butts and chains."

[90] Andrew Roche, "Gunbattles rage in Kabul, death toll over 100," Reuters, June 5, 1992.

[91] Cooperation Centre for Afghanistan, "The Prisoners and the Missing, Kabul, Afghanistan 1992-1995" (Peshawar: CCA, 1996).

[92] The name of this person has been changed to protect his security.

The number we put in the book was less, because we chose only the cases where we had some information about the how the people were kidnapped. There were more documents, with more information about the commanders, but we were pressed for time and we just published some of what we had.

It was very difficult to work on these issues at the time. One of our employees at the time was arrested by Harakat forces, and held for ransom, because of the research he was targeted. [Name deleted.] He was arrested in Dasht-e Barchi, sometime around the report research. He told us later that they beat him severely while he was held.[93]

H.K. said that the project staff tried to obtain the release of some of those who were held by the different forces:

Almost everyone we documented was never heard from again. However, in a few cases, rare cases, where we had all the information about who captured a person, and where they were held, we managed to get some people released. There was someone who worked with our information, and negotiated with Ittihad to get people released. That person negotiated with Sayyaf, [and later] with Ahmadzai [an Ittihad official who later served as prime minister].

All the commanders, in all the groups, would completely and totally deny that their forces were holding people. But in those rare cases where we had complete information about the detained person, and we confronted them with it, they would release the people. But this only happened in a few cases.

H.K. said that most of those who were released were tortured by their captors and exhibited physical signs of it. He told the story of one man he worked to have released, from Ittihad's forces, who said he had been forced to work "as a slave" on a commander's farm in Paghman. (The section "The Attack on Afshar" below contains addition information about forced labor).

We documented all of this. I interviewed him after he was released. He had been tortured by Ittihad when he was captured, and beaten severely

---

[93] Human Rights Watch interview with H.K., aid worker, Kabul, July 5, 2003.

in their prison. There were fifty other people being held with him, he said, somewhere in Paghman. After a few weeks, they sent him to this farm, to work on the land, during the day and night.

Former officials in the Rabbani government also supplied information to Human Rights Watch about Wahdat and Ittihad abductions, noting that commanders in Jamiat, Harakat, Junbish, and Hezb-e Islami sometimes detained civilians as well, usually just for ransom.[94] R.D., a former official in the interim government who was familiar with ongoing criminality by various factions, said that Anwar Dangar, a high-level commander in Shura-e Nazar, was "deeply involved in kidnapping schemes," and that another Jamiat commander, Kasim Jangal Bagh, was regularly implicated in abduction, or hostage-taking, for ransom.[95]

The research project noted above uncovered some of these abduction cases. As the researcher H.K. explained:

> Shura-e Nazar [meaning Jamiat forces under Massoud] arrested people as well. . . . In most cases, we were unable to do anything, but in three cases we managed to document what happened, and they released three people. They negotiated with the head of Amniat-e Melli [Afghan intelligence agency] at the time—Fahim [Mohammad Qasim Fahim]. To have them released they spoke with him.

Human Rights Watch also received testimony about abductions and killings of prisoners by Junbish forces in 1992 and 1993. Former Jamiat and Junbish officials confirmed to Human Rights Watch that Junbish forces regularly engaged in killings of prisoners in 1992 and 1993.[96]

---

[94] Human Rights Watch interview with S.A.R., former Shura-e Nazar official, Kabul, July 20, 2003; Human Rights Watch interview with C.S.A., former government security official, July 18, 2003.

[95] Human Rights Watch interview with R.D., former official in the interim government 1992-1995, Kabul, July 16, 2003. This was consistent with testimony by a former Shura-e Nazar official, Human Rights Watch interview with J.G.M., government security official in 1992-1993, Kabul, July 10, 2003.

[96] Human Rights Watch interview with U.J., former Junbish official, Kabul, July 13, 2003; Human Rights Watch interview with M.O.Q., former military official in Junbish, Kabul, July 17, 2003; Human Rights Watch interview with C.S.A., former government security official, July 18, 2003 (describing reports received by government officials about abuses by Junbish forces).

<u>Pillage and Looting</u>

Human Rights Watch interviewed scores of journalists, health workers, aid workers, taxi drivers, civil servants, and soldiers who witnessed widespread pillage and looting by Jamiat, Junbish, Wahdat, Ittihad, Harakat, and Hezb-e Islami forces after the Najibullah government fell.

Merchants in southeast Kabul told Human Rights Watch about looting by Hezb-e Islami forces in the area around Bala Hissar (southeast Kabul) in April 1992.[97] Embassies and diplomatic residencies were also reported to be targeted.[98] The U.N. human rights rapporteur for Afghanistan received reports that apartment complexes built for government employees in Micrayon were a focus of looting.[99] Journalists in Kabul covering the collapse of the old regime saw shops and houses being pillaged across the city.[100] An Afghan journalist described what he saw in April 1992:

> I saw with my own eyes Sayyaf's troops and Massoud's troops looting as they entered the city, breaking windows, stealing whatever they wanted. They were acting like animals, doing whatever they wanted.[101]

A BBC journalist described to Human Rights Watch looting he saw in May 1992:

> I saw General Dostum's Uzbek troops looting. . . . It was easy to recognize them. I knew who they were from their clothes and features. They were totally recognizable. I saw some of them carrying refrigerators on their backs, and

---

[97] Human Rights Watch interview with three merchants near Bala Hissar, Kabul, July 13, 2003 (describing Hezb-e Islami troops stealing from the bazaar).

[98] See Malcolm Davidson, "New government struggles to halt Kabul fighting," Reuters, April 30, 1992 and Sharon Herbaugh, "Anarchy rules in independent Afghanistan," Associated Press, June 1, 1992 (describing looting of diplomatic offices and residences).

[99] See Final Report on the Situation of Human Rights in Afghanistan, prepared by Felix Ermacora, Special Rapporteur on Afghanistan for the U.N. Commission on Human Rights, February 18, 1993, U.N. Document E/CN.4/1993/42, para. 19.

[100] Human Rights Watch interview with Steve Coll of the *Washington Post*, April 24, 2004; Human Rights Watch interview with Jeremy Bowen of the British Broadcasting Corporation, April 12, 2004; Human Rights Watch interview with Mark Urban of the British Broadcasting Corporation, April 29, 2004. See also, "Kabul leaders seek to restore city: but rocket attacks, looting go on as interim council meets," *Los Angeles Times*, May 1 1992. See also Derek Brown, "Rebel chief bombards Kabul homes," *The Guardian*, May 5, 1992; "Afghan city plagued by armed gangs," Reuters, June 20, 1992.

[101] Human Rights Watch interview with Y.U., Afghan journalist, Kabul, July 8, 2003.

other things like that, air conditioners. I remember especially some guys, Dostum's Uzbeks, coming out of a compound somewhere. These were happy and contented guys, smiling. They had some refrigerators and other appliances like that, carrying them on their backs. And I saw these smiling guys put the goods in their trucks and drive away. The Presidential Palace was looted by government troops [Jamiat and Junbish]. The troops went in, and were taking out carpets and things like that.[102]

Human Rights Watch received accounts that Dostum's highest military commanders in Kabul, including Majid Rouzi, were profiting from the looting by Junbish troops.[103]

General Abdul Rashid Dostum, leader of the Junbish faction, August 11, 1992. Junbish forces were implicated in war crimes and other abuses in Kabul in the early 1990s. As of mid-2005, Dostum holds a senior post in the ministry of defense. © 2001 Reuters Limited

A former official in Shura-e Nazar told Human Rights Watch about looting by Jamiat troops working for Kasim Jangal Bagh, a mid-level Jamiat commander:

---

[102] Human Rights Watch telephone interview with Jeremy Bowen, correspondent with the British Broadcasting Corporation in Kabul in 1992, April 12, 2004. Mark Urban, another journalist with BBC, also told Human Rights Watch about looting in April and May of 1992, Human Right Watch telephone interview with Mark Urban, correspondent with the British Broadcasting Corporation, April 29, 2004.

[103] Human Rights Watch interview with U.J., former Junbish official, July 13, 2003. This is consistent with testimony taken from another official in the interim government in 1992-1993: Human Rights Watch interview with C.S.A., former government security official, July 18, 2003.

Kasim Jangal Bagh's troops were responsible for the trouble that went on in [Micrayon and Wazir Akbar Khan—two neighborhoods in eastern Kabul]: looting, kidnapping, and raping of girls. . . . Kasim had a Ghund [military post]—it was independent I think. Bismullah Khan [a Shura-e Nazar commander] was his operational commander, but he may have reported directly to Massoud. . . . Massoud was giving him money [to pay his troops], but he was taking it for himself. I know—I know how these things work even now. He had cars, houses, but his gunmen were poor. So they were taking whatever they wanted from people. The soldiers were not paid, so they were robbing.[104]

A photojournalist who worked in Kabul through 1992 described seeing blocks of houses in west Kabul that were looted by Jamiat forces: "You'd notice blocks getting hit. Roof beams were torn out of the houses, electricity wires torn out, appliances, all the possessions."[105]

When questioned in late May 1992 about the looting, Commander Muslim, a senior official in the Jamiat faction and ostensibly in the Afghan ministry of defense, told a journalist, "Every society has its thieves and robbers. Ours is no different. Yes, there's chaos, yes there's disorder. But it's no worse than Los Angeles."[106] This was a reference to the large-scale riots and looting which had broken out in late April 1992 in Los Angeles, California, after a jury acquitted several police officers who had been videotaped beating an African-American motorist named Rodney King.

But Kabul was not Los Angeles. Many Kabul residents told Human Rights Watch that a culture of total impunity and chaos had come over Kabul in 1992, and that there was a general sense that the militia troops could do whatever they wanted at any time. Besides pillage and looting, there were regular incidents of killings and other violence.

A journalist with the British Broadcasting Corporation told Human Rights Watch about Junbish forces targeting civilians in April of 1992:

---

[104] Human Rights Watch interview with J.G.M., former official in Shura-e Nazar 1992-1996, Kabul, July 10, 2003.

[105] Human Rights Watch interview with R.N., photojournalist, New York, December 18, 2004.

[106] Herbaugh, "Anarchy rules in independent Afghanistan," June 1, 1992.

Junbish had been looting. . . . We filmed Junbish troops beating up this guy who had a bicycle. I guess they wanted to take the bicycle. I think that this was one of those rare cases where the presence of a camera literally stopped someone from being killed. They were clubbing him with Kalashnikovs, but when one of the troops saw us and pointed at us, they sent the guy on his way.

In another case, near the Intercontinental [Hotel], the camera led to problems. These Uzbek troops [Junbish] saw us, and they were acting up for the camera. They had this guy, this civilian, and they wanted to show off. They were making him stand a few meters away and they were shooting at his feet with their Kalashnikovs, making him dance. They were yelling, "Dance! Dance!" and shooting at his feet.[107]

Human Rights Watch documented several cases of killings by Junbish, Jamiat, and Harakat forces during 1992-1993. Former officials in Junbish and Jamiat admitted to Human Rights Watch that military forces in their former factions engaged in killings connected to pillage and looting.[108]

A Junbish official detailed some of the specific commanders involved in abuses:

Shir Arab, Ismail Diwaneh ["Ismail the Mad"], and Abdul Cherik[109] from the beginning engaged in widespread looting of the market. Killing took place only over looting. In late 1371, early 1372 [January to May 1993], they looted the Porzeforooshi Bazaar. . . . Ismail Diwaneh was in Bala Hissar [on the southeast edge of Kabul]. He regularly killed and robbed Pashtuns from Paktia who were passing through on the way to Kabul.[110]

---

[107] Human Rights Watch telephone interview with Mark Urban, correspondent with the British Broadcasting Corporation, April 29, 2004.

[108] Human Rights Watch interview with U.J., former Junbish official, Kabul, July 13, 2003; Human Rights Watch interview with M.O.Q., former military official in Junbish, Kabul, July 17, 2003; Human Rights Watch interview with J.G.M., former government security official in 1992-1993, Kabul, July 10, 2003; and Human Rights Watch interview with S.A.R., former Shura-e Nazar official, Kabul, July 11 and 20, 2003.

[109] These are the names of three Junbish commanders in 1992-1993, of whom only Shir Arab is still alive. The witness cited here told Human Rights Watch that he currently lives in Denmark.

[110] Human Rights Watch interview with M.O.Q., Kabul, July 17, 2003

Another former Shura-e Nazar official, discussing general looting by Jamiat forces in 1992 and 1993, described a particularly bad commander, Rahim "Kung Fu," who the official said was "a robber and killer and a thief, in a word, a criminal."[111] The official (who began crying as he was interviewed about Rahim) also told Human Rights Watch that Rahim was involved in killings of Hazara civilians, and children, during an operation against Wahdat forces posted in Timani neighborhood in 1992: "There were many rapes, the killing of many women and men. He was killing so many Hazaras. He killed children. I'm sorry, I cannot talk about it anymore."[112]

In a later interview, he described how he heard Rahim boast about crimes committed during the Taimani operation:

> He said he *pochaghed* Hazara [slaughtered, or cut their throats]. "We killed 300, 350 people," he said. "I went to a house. I saw an infant. I put the bayonet in its mouth. It sucked on it like a tit, then I pushed it through."[113]

One Kabul resident—a civil society organizer who often acted as a mediator between factions—told Human Rights Watch about an incident he witnessed in December 1992 when he said Junbish troops executed a Tajik man who had come to pay a ransom to release his brother, who he said was being held by a Junbish commander, Abdul Cherik:

> One day [a woman came to me] asking for a favor. [I] had a few connections with some people in Junbish, she was asking me to help her: her brother's car had been seized by some Junbish forces in December 1992. The car had been seized by Abdul Cherik—a commander with a checkpoint near the Kabul City Electrical Station (in east Kabul) in Chaman Waziri.
>
> I went to his checkpoint. While I was sitting there, waiting to talk to him [Cherik], a young guy, about 18 or 19, entered with a bag full of money. It was a Panshiri guy—I could tell because of his accent, and he looked Tajik.

---

[111] Human Rights Watch interview with S.A.R., former Shura-e Nazar official in 1992, Kabul, July 11, 2003.

[112] Ibid.

[113] Human Rights Watch interview with S.A.R., Kabul, July 20, 2003.

He asked Abdul Cherik to release his brother. He said: "This is the ransom you have asked for, for my brother," and he opened up the bag. It was full of money. I don't know how much.

Abdul Cherik looked at him, and then looked at his guards, and said, "Take him to his brother." And his guards motioned him to come, and they took his arm, and went out the back door. So they went out.

I was waiting in that room. About three minutes later, I heard the sound of gunshots, about fifty meters away. It was a burst of automatic gunfire. And then a little later, the gunmen came back in. They had some rings and a watch in their hands, and they gave Abdul Cherik the rings and watch, on his desk. I had gone to that place to try to convince this commander to release this guy's car, but after this happened, I immediately left the compound and walked away. I got outside and said to myself, "God save me," and left there.

I asked this guard near the door to the compound, "Did you kill him, or just take his rings and watch?" The Junbish guy said, "What a question! Can a Panshiri remain alive when he is imprisoned by us or is in our control?"

It was unimaginable to me that they would kill someone like that. It was something ordinary for them. You couldn't believe that they had killed him. It was like nothing had happened. The gunmen who were in the room there while I was waiting, they showed no reaction when those other men returned. It was an ordinary thing for them.[114]

A resident of Tiamani neighborhood of Kabul described a summary execution of a civilian by a Harakat soldier which he witnessed on a street in a neighborhood in north Kabul in September 1992:

I had [a store] in front of my house. I was selling some things there, one morning, sitting there. I saw this younger guy walk by—he had recently been married. Then I heard some shooting down the street. I looked down the street, and I saw that the guy who had passed was on the ground, and this other guy was over him—he held a pistol up to his

---

[114] Human Rights Watch interview with J.J.E, civil society leader, Kabul, July 10, 2003.

head and shot him in the temple. The guy was dead. Some other people on the street walked a little forward [i.e., toward the body, to look], and then stopped.[115]

The man said he did not know the reason for the killing, and did not know the name of the gunman but recognized him as someone he had seen with the Harakat faction:

This gunman, he was a Harakat gunman, just walked by us, slowly. Like he could do whatever he wanted. We saw him clearly. We knew who he was—he was a Harakat man.[116]

A Kabul resident, a bus driver, told Human Rights Watch about being arrested, having his bus stolen, and almost being executed by Hezb-e Islami forces, in late 1992:

One time, I was driving, and I had got to the end of my route, all the [passengers] had gotten off and the bus was empty. . . . A man and a teenager asked me to stop, and I slowed down, to give them a ride. Suddenly, armed men surrounded the truck, and got in, and ordered me to turn around, and when I hesitated, they beat me. So I turned around, and they made me go on a small road, toward Gardez. . . . They took me to this checkpost there—they were Hekmatyar's people. They made me show them how to use the car, the gears, and how to start it.

Then the commander said, "Take him to the mountain, and shoot him." And they started to lead me away. On the path [up the mountain], an old man saw me, and said, "What's the matter?" And I asked him to help me if he could. The troops pushed me forward. The old man went down to the commander [behind me] and told him not to kill me. [As an elder, the man presumably had additional influence.] The commander called up to the troops, "Just beat him." And that's what they did. They beat me very severely, and I lost consciousness. When I woke up, they had taken my watch, and I was alone. I went down the mountain on the other side, and got a cart to stop and take me into the

---

[115] Human Rights Watch interview with T.S.L., resident of Timani, Kabul, July 12, 2003.

[116] Ibid.

city. I got a rickshaw driver to take me to my house, but I fainted on the way, and my family had to carry me into my house. . . . [117]

Violations of International Humanitarian Law

As noted earlier in this report, the intentional targeting of civilians and civilian objects for attack is a violation of international humanitarian law that can amount to a war crime. In addition, article 3 common to the four Geneva Conventions, which is applicable in non-international armed conflicts, requires the humane treatment of civilians and detained combatants. Arbitrary deprivation of liberty, murder, torture, rape and other ill-treatment violate this requirement. International humanitarian law also prohibits "pillage," which is defined as the forcible taking of private property from an enemy's subjects, and other forms of theft.

Murder, adverse treatment and unlawful deprivation of liberty of civilians (as well as captured combatants), on the basis of their ethnicity or other distinction, violates common article 3 to the Geneva Conventions. Furthermore, widespread or systematic abductions, killings and "disappearances" that are part of an attack on a civilian population, such as an ethnic group, may amount to crimes against humanity.[118]

There is compelling evidence presented above that Ittihad and Wahdat forces abducted thousands of persons in the first year of the post-Najibullah era, as well as more in later years. The fact that so many persons arrested were never again seen by their families suggests that both the Ittihad and Wahdat factions killed thousands of these detainees. There is also compelling evidence that detainees who survived their detention were tortured or otherwise mistreated. The widespread murders, arbitrary deprivations of liberty, torture and other mistreatment committed by Ittihad and Wahdat forces may amount to war crimes and crimes against humanity.

Sayyaf, as the leader of Ittihad, is centrally implicated in the abuses described above, since he exercised ultimate control of Ittihad forces. Officials in the Rabbani government in 1992-1993, allied with Sayyaf, acknowledged to Human Rights Watch that Sayyaf, as the senior military commander of Ittihad forces, was in regular contact with his commanders, and that he had the power to release prisoners held by his subordinates, and in fact ordered such releases on several occasions, demonstrating his

---

[117] Human Rights Watch interview with F.R.G., Kabul resident, Kabul, July 3, 2003.

[118] For more on article 3 common to the Geneva Conventions and other specific prohibitions within international humanitarian law, see section IV below.

command over those commanders.[119] Health workers in west Kabul told Human Rights Watch in 2003 of additional cases in which negotiators with the International Committee of the Red Cross spoke with Sayyaf to obtain the release of prisoners, further demonstrating his control over subordinate commanders.[120] Human Rights Watch also spoke with an individual who negotiated with Sayyaf to obtain a relative's release.[121] And in June 1992, when interviewed by a journalist in Kabul about the abductions, Sayyaf did not deny that Ittihad forces were abducting Hazara civilians, but merely accused Wahdat of being an agent of the Iranian government.[122]

Further investigation will also be needed into other Ittihad commanders and their role in the abductions and abuses documented here. Investigations will need to focus in particular on the role of Ittihad commanders Shir Alam, Mullah Ezat, Zalmay Tofan, Abdul Manan, Dr. Abdullah, and Noor Aqa, who were named by several sources in this report as being implicated in abductions and holding of prisoners for forced labor.[123] More detailed discussion of the potential legal responsibility of Sayyaf and his other commanders, for the abuses described here and elsewhere in this report, is set forth in section IV below.

As for Wahdat, its leader, Mazari, who was killed in 1995, was implicated in the abuses above. Mazari and his deputy, Karim Khalili (now the vice-president of Afghanistan), acknowledged taking Pashtun civilians as prisoners in interviews with Reuters and Associated Press.[124] Mazari defended the practice by stating that Ittihad troops had first

---

[119] Human Rights Watch interview with S.A.R., former Shura-e Nazar official in 1992, Kabul, July 11, 2003; Human Rights Watch interview with R.D., former official in the interim government 1992-1995, Kabul, July 16, 2003; Human Rights Watch interview with C.S.A., former government security official, July 18, 2003.

[120] Human Rights Watch interview with H.K., aid worker, Kabul, July 5, 2003; Human Rights Watch interview with S.K., Afghan medical worker in Karte Seh (West Kabul) during early 1990's, Kabul, July 9, 2003.

[121] Human Rights Watch interview with L.R.G., Kabul, July 3, 2003.

[122] See Roche, "Kabul fighting erupts again despite ceasefire," Reuters, June 4, 1992

[123] "The Prisoners and the Missing," cited above, alleges that these commanders were responsible for many of the disappearances and abductions documented in that report.

[124] Andrew Roche, "Kabul fighting erupts again despite ceasefire," Reuters, June 4, 1992; Sharon Herbaugh, "Civilians tell of captivity, torture by rebels," Associated Press, June 6, 1992.

seized Hazaras.[125] (Mazari later said that detained prisoners were kept in houses, given food and water, and not tortured.[126])

Further investigation will be needed into the command-and-control structure of Wahdat and the culpability of the commanders who are still alive. More investigation is needed into Karim Khalili's involvement in military decision-making and his control over Wahdat forces. Shafi Dawana and Nasir Dawana have been killed, but Wahid Turkmani, Mohsin Sultani, Tahir Tofan, Sedaqat Jahori, and Commander Bahrami are believed to be still alive, and should also be investigated for their role in the Wahdat abuses documented here. The potential legal responsibility of Wahdat commanders for the abuses documented here is further discussed in section IV below.

In addition to the abductions and killings, the widespread looting and pillage that took place in Kabul during the period discussed above should also be investigated. Troops or commanders from all the factions named above who were involved in pillage need to be thoroughly investigated.

Rape and Sexual Violence

Several health workers in Kabul who spoke with Human Rights Watch stated that rape and other forms of sexual violence were commonly committed against women who were abducted by Wahdat and Ittihad forces in 1992-1993, as well as generally during the hostilities around Kabul at the time.[127] Human Rights Watch was unable to obtain direct accounts from victims of rape during this period, in large part due to deep reluctance among women and girls to grant interviews on the subject, or refusals by families of the victims to allow such interviews. But there is evidence of its occurrence. H.K., who worked on a documentation project into abductions discussed earlier in this report, told Human Rights Watch that researchers working on this issue in the early 1990's knew of widespread abductions and rape of women in west Kabul, although he said that families were in most cases unwilling to give information about details:

---

[125] Roche, "Kabul fighting erupts again despite ceasefire," June 4, 1992. Under article 3 common to the four Geneva Conventions of 1949, parties to non-international armed conflicts have no right to resort to reprisals, defined as normally unlawful acts used by a belligerent to force the enemy to respect international humanitarian law. For instance, common article 3 prohibits inhumane treatment such as abductions "at any time and in any place whatsoever."

[126] Herbaugh, "Civilians tell of captivity, torture by rebels," June 6, 1992.

[127] Human Rights Watch interview with S.K., Afghan medical worker, Kabul, July 9, 2003; Human Rights Watch interview with H.K., aid worker, Kabul, July 5, 2003.

It was impossible to document the rape or kidnapping of women in these cases. The families always denied cases where the women were kidnapped or raped, because of the dishonor and shame. The families would deny that their women were kidnapped, or refuse to discuss these cases; it is because Afghan families are very conservative. There would be lots of stories, lots of talk about how "other families" had had the women abducted. A set of people would tell us, "Look, that family over there, across the street, their women were kidnapped," but when we went over to ask the family themselves, they would deny it, and say nothing had happened. This is how it always happened. Maybe they would admit it if a boy was abducted, for rape, but not the women.[128]

Human Rights Watch did receive accounts from several journalists and civil society organizers about cases of rape which they documented—specifically, cases of troops from Jamiat, Hezb-e Islami, and Wahdat breaking into houses and raping women.[129] Human Rights Watch also received credible information from government sources about cases of rape by Jamiat, Wahdat, and Junbish forces.[130] S.K., the health worker in west Kabul quoted earlier, said she treated numerous women who said they had been raped by militia forces in west Kabul in 1992-1993, and collected bodies of women in the streets who showed signs of having been raped.[131]

---

[128] Human Rights Watch interview with H.K., aid worker, Kabul, July 5, 2003.

[129] 'Human Rights Watch interview with Y.U., journalist, Kabul, July 8, 2003 (documented rape of women by Hezb-e Islami forces); Human Rights Watch interview with J.J.E, civil society leader, Kabul, July 10, 2003 (documented case of three women raped by Jamiat forces in Micrayon); Human Rights Watch telephone interview with John Jennings, Associated Press correspondent in Kabul 1992-1993, April 8, 2004 (describing evidence of rape by Wahdat). Terence White, a journalist with Agence France-Presse, also documented cases of rape of Afghan women by various mujahedin forces in 1992 and 1993. See Terence White, "Afghan women protest outside UN office as Turks evacuate Kabul," Agence France-Presse, February 9, 1993.

[130] Human Rights Watch interview with J.G.M., former government security official in 1992-1993, Kabul, July 10, 2003 and Human Rights Watch interview with S.A.R., former Shura-e Nazar official, Kabul, July 11 and 20, 2003 (admitting Jamiat forces were regularly implicated in rapes); Human Rights Watch interview with K.M.B., former combatant who served under Ittihad forces, Kabul, July 4, 2003 (witnessed women who said they were raped by Wahdat); Human Rights Watch interview with C.S.A., former government security official, July 18, 2003 (documented rapes by Junbish).

[131] Human Rights Watch interview with S.K., Afghan medical worker in west Kabul during early 1990's, Kabul, July 9, 2003. S.K. described a typical case of a woman she found on the street in Karte She, in west Kabul: "A Pashtun; she had some tattoos on her face. She had been killed, and she had been tortured, you could see, and raped. We picked her up and took her to the hospital. . . ." Ibid.

More investigation is needed to determine the scope of rape as a practice among the various troops in Kabul in the post-Najibullah period. Based on the available information, rape may have been a chronic problem in Kabul during the period and numerous commanders, including at the highest levels of each faction, appear to have failed to take appropriate steps to prevent further cases from occurring. In some cases, sub-commanders themselves may have been involved in rapes.[132]

B: October 1992–February 1993

Kabul suffered relatively less intense fighting after the August 1992 blitz on the city, but serious firefights and shelling rocked the city throughout the later part of the year.

In October, the leadership council set up under the Peshawar accords voted to extend Rabbani's term for forty-five days, until December, on the grounds that the summer fighting had made the summoning of the council impossible. Jamiat forces repeatedly battled Wahdat in the west, near Kabul University, causing further casualties and damage. At the same time, there were increasing signs that Dostum's Junbish faction was starting to negotiate with Hekmatyar's Hezb-e Islami, despite the fact Hekmatyar had initially opposed Dostum, and used Dostum's presence in Kabul (as a former communist government official) as a pretext for opposing Massoud.

In December 1992, Rabbani convened the council of representatives called for under the Peshawar Accords to choose the next government—or just reelect him as president.[133] The council, however, was not representative of the different warring factions or the general Afghan population. Many of the invited members boycotted the vote, including representatives of Junbish, Wahdat and Hezb-e Islami. Rabbani was "reelected" by his supporters, allies and proxies in the meeting, and stated his intention to serve as president for another 18 months. Hekmatyar, however, refused to accept the outcome of the council, and vowed to dislodge Rabbani's government, and Massoud's forces, in the coming months. Wahdat rejected the new government as well, and soon made an official alliance with Hekmatyar. Junbish, for the most part, stayed on the sidelines.[134]

---

[132] For more information on the specific legal standards of international humanitarian law applicable to rape and the culpability of individual commanders, see section IV below.

[133] For an account of this meeting, see Sayyid Alamuddin Assir, *Elal-e Soghoot-e Dolat-e Islami-e Afghanistan Taht-e Ghiyadat-e Ustad Rabbani dar Kabul* ("*The Reasons for the Fall of the Islamic State of Afghanistan Under the Rule of Ustad Rabbani in Kabul*") (likely Peshawar: publisher unknown, 2001).

[134] Assir, *Elal-e Soghoot*, pp. 91-103; Sangar, *Neem Negahi Bar E'telafhay-e Tanzimi dar Afghanistan*, pp. 162-167.

Burhanuddin Rabbani, seated, the political leader of Jamiat-e Islami and President of Afghanistan after Mujaddidi. © 1992 Robert Nickelsberg

January – February 1993: Conflict Continues

Fighting between Jamiat and Hezb-e Islami/Wahdat flared up the week of January 19, 1993. Jamiat forces attacked several Hezb-e Islami positions to the south and southeast of Kabul early in the week, and Hekmatyar's forces soon restarted rocket and shelling attacks on the city center.[135] Heavy fighting broke out later in the week between Wahdat and Jamiat forces in west Kabul, near the Intercontinental Hotel and the large agricultural compound west of Mamorine neighborhood, known as "the Silo," as well as in other places in the west. Wahdat and Hizb-e Islami forces were now cooperating.[136]

In statements given to journalists, the two opposing sides—Jamiat on one side and Wahdat and Hizb-e Islami on the other—blamed the other for the resumption in hostilities.[137]

---

[135] This account of the first three weeks of fighting in Kabul, starting the week of January 19, 1993, is based on extensive interviews with witnesses to the fighting, aid workers, Afghan and international journalists, officials in the various factions, and other witnesses knowledgeable about the events.

[136] Yunis Qanooni, in 1993 a senior official in Jamiat and the government defense ministry under Massoud, told journalists in Kabul the first week of February that Wahdat and Hezb-e Islami were now loosely aligned with each other.

[137] Terence White, "Rebel faction holds out under pressure from government," Agence France-Presse, January 20, 1993 ("government" and "Hezb" officials quoted); Terence White, "South Kabul under

Over the next three weeks, thousands of Kabul residents were wounded and killed in the fighting, according to health officials interviewed by Human Rights Watch and others who spoke with journalists at the time. Some of the last diplomatic offices in Kabul were evacuated, including the Turkish, Iranian, Chinese, and Indian embassies.

The fighting grew worse as weeks passed. Journalists working in Kabul at the time told Human Rights Watch that the hospitals they visited were constantly full, with scores of wounded civilians and soldiers brought in daily. Many of the dead were never brought to hospitals at all. A journalist recalled the general level of chaos at the time, and driving from the city center to west Kabul to see the fighting:

> It was complete madness. No one was on the roads. On the main road [running to Darulman in west Kabul] there were rockets coming in all around. It was terrifying really. It wasn't really possible to tell where they were coming from.

> When you went down to Charasyab [southwest of Kabul] you'd see rocket launchers, where Hekmatyar's troops were. And on that mountain behind Wazir [Bibi Mahru hill] also. . . . There were attacks all the time. It was completely arbitrary whether you could get to the places that had been hit quickly enough to cover it [interview people and file stories]. We saw terrible things. Dead people, wounded people, corpses on the side of the road. One time we saw the remains of a child, lying on the ground. One time we picked up a guy who had been wounded, a civilian, with a huge hole in his side. It was horrible really. We had to put him in the boot of the car and we drove him to the hospital. It was quite absurd. I don't think that he lived. . .[138]

intense rebel bombardment, many casualties," Agence France-Presse, January 21, 1993 (quoting "government" officials); Suzy Price, "Hundreds of casualties in Afghan fighting," Reuters, January 21, 1993 (quoting "government" and "Hezb" statements); and Suzy Price, "Rebel Afghan chief attacks Kabul for the 19th day," Reuters, February 6, 1993 (quoting Yunis Qanooni and Abul Ali Mazari).

[138] Human Rights Watch interview with Suzy Price, correspondent for the British Broadcasting Corporation and Reuters, New York, April 1, 2004.

Many of the rockets and shells fired by both sides were clearly hitting civilian areas on a regular basis, and most of the patients brought to the hospitals mentioned above were in fact civilians.[139]

There is no accurate tally of dead and wounded civilians during the fighting, but journalists in Kabul at the time were able to gather limited reports day-to-day:

- On January 19, a health official reported to Agence France-Presse that 33 wounded persons had been brought to a central hospital, of whom eight died.[140]

- On February 4, according to reports gathered by the Reuters journalist quoted above, at least 41 persons were admitted to one hospital in Wazir Akbar Khan, 10 persons died at a nearby military hospital (with "many more" injured) and at the Jamhuriat hospital, there were 26 wounded admitted, of whom four died.[141] Dr. Said Omar, a doctor at Jamhuriat, told the journalist: "This is heavy artillery and it totally cuts up the bodies. . . . This is the worst morning we have had."[142]

- On February 8, 1993, Hezb-e Islami and Wahdat forces fired rockets and artillery at Jamiat positions throughout the day, including in civilian areas in the eastern and central parts of the city, while Jamiat positions on Bibi Mahru hill, behind the Wazir Akbar Khan neighborhood, fired rockets at Hezb-e Islami positions to the south.[143] Scores of shells and rockets fell in the city: in Micrayon, Wazir Akbar Khan, West Kabul, Afshar, and neighborhoods on the lower part of Television Mountain, killing and injuring hundreds of people. There was also fighting between Jamiat and Hezb-e Islami in and near the

---

[139] Human Rights Watch telephone interview with Marc Biot, official at Jamhuriat hospital in Kabul in 1992-1993, July 10, 2004; Human Rights Watch interview with S.K., Afghan medical worker in west Kabul during early 1990's, Kabul, July 9, 2003.

[140] Terence White, "Rocket attack kills eight, Afghan troops suffer heavy losses," Agence France-Presse, January 19, 1993 (quoting hospital officials).

[141] Suzy Price, "Hospitals full as more rockets hit Afghan capital," Reuters, February 4, 1993; Human Rights Watch interviews with Suzy Price, New York, March 2004.

[142] Ibid.

[143] This account of February 8, 1993 is based on newswire stories filed by international journalists in Kabul and interviews with some of those journalists: Human Rights Watch interview with Suzy Price, correspondent for the British Broadcasting Corporation and Reuters, New York, April 3, 2004, Human Rights Watch telephone interviews with John Jennings, April 8 and 10, 2004. See also, Terence White, "Kabul pounded by rocket fire," Agence France-Presse, February 8, 1993; John Jennings, "Fighting intensifies in Afghan capital," Associated Press, February 8, 1993; Suzy Price, "Dozens killed, hurt in shelling of Afghan capital," Reuters, February 8, 1993.

Russian Embassy and the Presidential Palace. That day, a hospital in Wazir Akbar Khan reported 20 dead and 60 wounded; a journalist saw the hallways filled with groaning patients with shrapnel wounds, and dead bodies in the parking lot. Dr. Mohammad Qasem told the journalist: "This is the highest number since the fighting began."[144] Medical staff at other hospitals couldn't count the bodies that day: "We don't have time to count them, we're too busy trying to look after them," a nurse at the Jamhuriat hospital told another journalist.[145]

By the end of the first week of February, medical staff in Kabul reported 800 deaths and 3,500 to 4,000 injuries since January 19, 1993—a three week period—while pointing out that the number of dead was likely much higher, since most families were not bringing the civilian dead to hospitals or reporting deaths.[146] Armin Kobel, the chief of ICRC, told journalists that 368 wounded were admitted to Kabul's hospitals February 10.[147] On February 12, a doctor at an ICRC hospital told an Agence France-Presse journalist that the total dead citywide in the period (civilian and combatants) was probably around 5,000.[148]

A Kabul resident who was present in West Kabul at the time of the fighting told Human Rights Watch:

> It was a terrible time. There were rockets coming every day. During the night, bullets and artillery would be launched from Qargha from the west [area on the border of Paghman district to the west of Kabul, controlled by Jamiat and Sayyaf's Ittihad forces]. And from the mountain, Mamorine [controlled by Jamiat], came shells. They were shelling from Mamorine, into Afshar, hitting the side of mountain. We lived in the basement during this time. . . .[149]

---

[144] Price, "Dozens killed, hurt in shelling of Afghan capital," February 8, 1993.

[145] Jennings, "Fighting intensifies in Afghan capital," February 8, 1993.

[146] Price, "Dozens killed, hurt in shelling of Afghan capital," February 8, 1993; Jennings, "Fighting intensifies in Afghan capital," February 8, 1993.

[147] Terence White, "Former Pakistan secret service chief arrives in Kabul," Agence France-Presse, February 10, 1993 (quoting Kobel).

[148] Terence White, "No respite in Kabul rocket barrage, death toll close to 5,000," Agence France-Presse, February 12, 1993.

[149] Human Rights Watch interview with L.M., resident of Afshar, Kabul, July 12, 2003.

Another witness, a doctor who was a medical student at a hospital at the time, told Human Rights Watch about the situation in both West Kabul and the central city:

> There was a lot of fighting going on in our neighborhood around this time. There were many times I saw fighting like this. We saw terrible rocketing and shelling, by Shura-e Nazar and by Hekmatyar. Rockets hitting hospitals; people would be broken into pieces: hands, feet, heads.

> One time, a rocket flew in and exploded at the Amniat hospital, where we were studying at the time because of the insecurity at the main university. It was about ten in the morning. . . . Some doctors died, some of the female students died, one girl went crazy, from an injury to her head. One girl lost her eyes. I myself saw all of this—the damage after the rocket hit: people torn into pieces. Many people were killed by that rocket. It came from the west, over television mountain [the main peak in central Kabul, suggesting it was fired from Hekmatyar's positions in southwest Kabul].[150]

A resident of Afshar in West Kabul told Human Rights Watch how his brother and later his father were killed by shelling and rockets in his neighborhood in late January 1993:

> One early morning [the last week of January], while I was still asleep, my older brother went down to a well below our house [down the mountain] to get some water for the family. . . . Later, the neighbors woke us, telling us to come down to this shop . . . . We went down: there were seven or eight corpses, lined up near this store there. We were told that a rocket had hit near to the well, and my brother had been killed. There were explosions all the time in those days. . . .

> We couldn't bury him, it was so unsafe to be outside for too long. . . . That night, we took him out to bury him near to our house. We brought a hurricane lamp with us, but didn't light it. It was quiet, as we dug a hole and the cleric with us spoke and we prayed. Then we lit the hurricane lamp, in order to lower him into the ground. As soon as we lit that hurricane lamp, we heard them firing from Mamorine [the mountain southeast of Afshar, held by Jamiat], and explosions hit nearby, so we extinguished the light and buried him in the dark. It was

---

[150] Human Rights Watch interview with F.K.Z., resident of west Kabul, Kabul, July 9, 2003.

Shura-e Nazar [Jamiat forces]. They would shoot at us from Mamorine all the time—at ordinary civilians. They would shoot at anyone, but especially crowds of four or more.[151]

The man's father was killed in an attack three days later:

> It was morning, and we thought we could go out, it was quiet. We needed some food. So my father went out. As he was going down the steps, in the mountain, a rocket hit very near to him. My father collapsed. We went to him. Shrapnel had hit him. He was seriously wounded. We started to carry him, to get a way to go to the hospital. But he was bleeding so much, and it didn't stop. He bled to death. . . . When we had to bury him, we faced the same difficulties as with my brother.[152]

Thousands of civilians fled their homes in Kabul throughout late January and early February. Human Rights Watch interviewed several men who sent their families out of Kabul during this time, complaining of the constant fighting. "We left because there was heavy shelling and a lot of shooting, with heavy weapons," one man who fled in early February told Human Rights Watch.[153] "Sakr [Soviet-made] rockets were flying into the area [west Kabul]. . . . The artillery and rockets were hitting the houses, indiscriminately. We didn't feel safe, so we left."[154] Journalists in Kabul at the time reported seeing families fleeing on roads out of the city. One man shouted to journalists as he pushed a cart with his belongings out of the city on February 9: "These mujahedin are taking us back to the first century!"[155]

C: February 1993: the Afshar Campaign

The Wahdat and Hezb-e Islami alliance was a new threat to the Rabbani government, since Wahdat already held positions in central Kabul itself, including much of west Kabul and areas between the eastern portions of the city, where most government buildings were located, and the western hills of Paghman, where Sayyaf and his Ittihad

---

[151] Human Rights Watch interview with Y.B.K., former resident of Afshar as a young boy, Kabul, July 11, 2003.

[152] Ibid.

[153] Human Rights Watch interview with A.S.F., resident of west Kabul, July 2, 2003.

[154] Ibid.

[155] Suzy Price, "Afghans flee Kabul during lull in shelling," Reuters, February 9, 1993.

militia were headquartered. Wahdat's possession of the peak of Afshar mountain, north of the main road to Paghman, made their position especially strong.

In early February 1993, the government of Burhanuddin Rabbani and the senior Jamiat and Ittihad commanders decided to take action against the Wahdat and Hezb-e Islami alliance by attacking Wahdat's main positions in the west of the city and, in particular, their positions on the top of Afshar mountain and in several government compounds to the east of the Afshar residential area at the foot of the mountain.

Human Rights Watch received credible and consistent accounts from several officials who worked in Shura-e Nazar and the interim government that a military campaign against Wahdat was planned and approved by officials at the highest levels of Jamiat and Shura-e Nazar, Ittihad, and the Rabbani government.[156]

The plan was for a coordinated military attack on Wahdat headquarters located in the Academy of Social Science, near the Polytechnic University, at the foot of the Afshar neighborhood in west Kabul. The specific objectives of the campaign were for Jamiat and Ittihad forces to seize and occupy the headquarters and main Wahdat positions around Afshar so that the government forces could link up their control of Kabul from the west (around Paghman district) to the eastern parts of the city, and to capture the political and military leader of Wahdat, Abdul Ali Mazari.

The Afghan Justice Project, the independent non-governmental group that investigated the Afshar incident and other military operations in Afghanistan from 1979 through 2001, described the operation in a January 2005 report:

> The Afshar operation of February 1993 represented the largest and most integrated use of military power undertaken by the ISA up to that time [ISA refers to the Islamic State of Afghanistan, the Rabbani-led government]. There were two tactical objectives to the operation. First, Massoud intended through the operation to capture the political and military headquarters of Hizb-i Wahdat, (which was located in the Social Science Institute, adjoining Afshar, the neighborhood below the Afshar

---

[156] Human Rights Watch interview with K.S., former government security official, Kabul, July 24, 2003; Human Rights Watch interview with C.S.A., former government security official, July 18, 2003; Human Rights Watch interview with R.D., former official in the interim government 1992-1995, Kabul, July 16, 2003; Human Rights Watch interview with J.G.M., former government intelligence official 1992-1996, Kabul, July 10, 2003. Intelligence agents in Wahdat also told Human Rights Watch that they knew in advance of an impending attack by Jamiat and Ittihad forces.

mountain in west Kabul), and to capture Abdul Ali Mazari, the leader of Hizb-i Wahdat. Second, the ISA intended to consolidate the areas of the capital directly controlled by Islamic State forces by linking up parts of west Kabul controlled by Ittihad-i Islami with parts of central Kabul controlled by Jamiat-i Islami.[157]

The attack was not a well-kept secret among the militias. Wahdat political officials knew that an offensive was planned several days before it began, as did a small number of well-connected Afshar residents, who fled in the days before the attack.[158] A few Afshar residents who received word of an impending attack were able to leave. A resident described to Human Rights Watch how he learned of the attack:

> A friend of mine, he was involved in Shura-e Nazar. He worked in the headquarters and in the government. He came to me, before the invasion, two days before, and he said, "You must get out of here. There is an order for an invasion. Paghmani people [Ittihad] will attack this area, kill everyone, and loot every house."[159]

Another said:

> A family relation we had, who was a fighter with Massoud, told us to leave. He said to us, 'Sayyaf's people and Massoud's people are going to attack here.' This was four days before. He told us to leave. So we left.[160]

And another:

> Five days before the attack, a nephew of mine who was a bodyguard for Anwari [Harakat's leader] came and told me: "You should get out of here, this place will collapse. And even if you are not a combatant, there will be lots of destruction." Two days later, at night, we left.[161]

---

[157] Afghan Justice Project, "Addressing the Past: The Legacy of War Crimes and the Political Transition in Afghanistan," January 2005, ("AJP report"), page 27.

[158] Human Rights Watch interview with Q.E.K., former Wahdat political official, Kabul, July 15, 2003.

[159] Human Rights Watch interview with I.R.H., resident of Afshar, Kabul, July 12, 2003.

[160] Human Rights Watch interview with I.K., resident of Afshar, Kabul, July 2, 2003.

[161] Human Rights Watch interview with K.I.K., resident of Afshar, Kabul, July 6, 2003.

Most residents in the area, however, were not aware of the impending operation and were not warned or evacuated.[162]

The operation's key was the top of Afshar mountain itself, lying above Afshar neighborhood. The military strategy centered around Jamiat taking control of the peaks of the mountain, before moving on Wahdat positions at the southeast base of the hill, to the east of Afshar's civilian area.[163] Just before the attack, agents in the Jamiat-controlled Afghan intelligence service, or *Amniat-e Melli*, headed by Mohammad Fahim (Afghanistan's defense minister from 2001-2004 and a key military ally of the United States during operations against the Taliban in late 2001) paid off several Harakat faction commanders to the north and west of Afshar, to cooperate with the invasion and allow Jamiat and Ittihad troops to pass their posts unmolested and to seize Afshar's peak.[164] When the attack later began, Jamiat forces did seize Afshar's peak, and Ittihad entered Afshar itself and took control of Wahdat positions at the Academy of Social Science and along the road that runs south of Afshar from Paghman into central Kabul. Jamiat forces also took positions on the roads leading in and out of Afshar. Wahdat forces, meanwhile, fled south into west Kabul, leaving the predominately Hazara civilian population of Afshar in the hands of the predominately Pashtun Ittihad troops.

Two days before the attack, Massoud convened a meeting at the military base at Badambagh in Kabul, comprised of senior commanders in Jamiat and Ittihad, and other commanders within the overall structure of Shura-e Nazar.[165] The senior leadership of

---

[162] Several residents told Human Rights Watch they had not been prepared to evacuate; e.g., Human Rights Watch interview with F.A., woman from Afshar, Kabul, July 6, 2003 ("I didn't know that the top of the mountain had been sold to Massoud.").

[163] The general descriptions of the Afshar campaign here are based on testimony taken by researchers with the Afghan Justice Project, as well as Human Rights Watch interviews with officials named in the proceeding note, and interviews with two soldiers who took part in the Afshar campaign; Human Rights Watch interview with K.M.B., soldier who served under Ittihad forces in 1993, Kabul, July 4, 2003 (describing his orders on the day of the attack) and Human Rights Watch interview with T.E.S., soldier in Shura-e Nazar in 1993, Kabul, July 5, 2003 (describing aim of attack on Afshar as told to him by his commanders).

[164] The Harakat and Wahdat commanders alleged to have received payments from Jamiat were Sadaqat, Zabit Mohsin Sultani, Iwaz Ali Ghorjai, Tabbish, Malik Sherif, and Sayyid Sherif. Human Rights Watch received consistent testimony on these names from former officials in Wahdat and Shura-e Nazar. Human Rights Watch interview with Q.Q.S., former Wahdat commander, Kabul, July 14, 2004; Human Rights Watch interview with Q.E.K., former Wahdat political official, Kabul, July 15, 2003; Human Rights Watch interview with C.S.A., former government security official, July 18, 2003.

[165] See AJP report, January 2005, p. 29.

Jamiat at the time included Mullah Ezat (Ezatullah), a commander in Paghman; Mohammad Qasim Fahim (the head of Amniat-e Melli); Baba Jan; Anwar Dangar; Gadda Mohammad; Baba Jalander; Haji Almas; Gul Haider, and Bismillah Khan.

Human Rights Watch was unable to confirm exactly who was at this meeting, but it is almost certain that Fahim was there, given the importance of his role in organizing the preparation for the operation. According to a witness interviewed by the Afghan Justice Project, two senior Ittihad commanders—Shir Alam and Zalmay Tofan—were at the meeting, as well as Hossain Anwari, leader of the Harakat faction.[166]

The next day, Sayyaf reportedly met with senior Ittihad commanders in Paghman to discuss the planned attack.[167] Ittihad's leadership at the time included Sayyaf himself, Haji Shir Alam, Zalmay Tufan, Abdullah Shah, and Mullah Taj Mohammad. Several mid-level commanders were probably also at the meeting.

Another commanders' meeting was held by Massoud in a safe house in Karte Parwan, near the Hotel Intercontinental, on the night before the offensive.[168] According to the Afghan Justice Project, Massoud also convened a meeting in the Hotel Intercontinental on the second day of the operation, February 12, attended by military commanders and political figures, including Rabbani, Sayyaf and Fahim.[169]

Human Rights Watch interviewed numerous residents in Afshar who were present at the time who described how the attack and its aftermath unfolded. As shown here, there is credible and consistent evidence of widespread and systematic human rights abuses and violations of international humanitarian law during and after the Afshar operation, including intentional killing of civilians, beating of civilians, abductions based on ethnicity, looting, and forced labor. The widespread and deliberate nature of these attacks suggests that some of the commanders involved in these abuses could be liable for crimes against humanity.

Artillery Attacks

Before the actual ground attack, Jamiat forces positioned new artillery on the peaks of Aliabad hill and Mamorine mountain, nearby; Ittihad already had artillery and rocket

---

[166] Ibid.

[167] AJP report, p. 29.

[168] Ibid.

[169] AJP report, January 2005, p. 30.

launchers in place at Qargha, on the Paghman border to the west of Afshar. Journalists and military officials familiar with the operation believe the weapons deployed on Mamorine and Television Mountains, at the Hotel Intercontinental, and at the Kabul Zoo included BM-40, BM-22, and BM-12 rocket launchers (mounted cubes of 12), Sakr 18 rocket launchers, 120mm mortars, 82mm mortars, and D30 (or "DC") 105mm cannons. Jamiat forces also put tanks in various areas to use their cannon fire.[170]

There was periodic artillery and rocket fire directed at the Afshar area February 7-10. According to residents who lived in Afshar at the time, ordinance fell repeatedly on the civilian homes below the top of Afshar mountain and to the west and northwest of Mazari's headquarters at the Academy of Social Science.[171] A resident who was wounded at the time told Human Rights Watch about the effects of the initial artillery fire:

> They [referring to Ittihad and Jamiat] were firing at the top of the hill [Afshar]. . . . Mostly the artillery was falling into this area. Many houses were hit. Our house was hit during this time.
>
> I remember: I heard my son shriek. I was wounded also, in the torso here, in the stomach. My granddaughter was also killed by the same shell, and my other daughter was wounded in the face and disfigured. My house was on fire. Three or four other houses were hit as well around here [gesturing in a circle].[172]

Another resident, J.L.S., saw the beginning of the attack: "My house is at the foot of the mountain. I woke up early on the morning of the attack, to take ablution for prayer. Suddenly, there was a lot of artillery firing. I looked up toward the communication

---

[170] Human Rights Watch telephone interview with John Jennings, Associated Press correspondent in Kabul 1992-1993, April 10, 2004 (observed weapons deployments); Human Rights Watch interview with Q.E.K., former political official in Wahdat who observed attack from west Kabul, Kabul, July 15, 2003; testimony of a military official interviewed by the Afghan Justice Project, see AJP report, January 2005, p. 29.

[171] Human Rights Watch interview with A.S.F., Tajik man from Afshar, Kabul, July 2, 2003; Human Rights Watch interview with F.K.M., Afshar resident, Kabul, July 2, 2003; Human Rights Watch interview with B.O.Q., Afshar resident, Kabul, July 6, 2003; Human Rights Watch interview with I.A.S.M., Afshar resident, Kabul, July 6, 2003; Human Rights Watch interview with L.M., Afshar resident, Kabul, July 12, 2003; Human Rights Watch interview with A.Q.L., Afshar resident, July 21, 2003; Human Rights Watch interview with Q.L.N., Afshar resident, Kabul, July 23, 2003.

[172] Human Rights Watch interview with F.K.M., Afshar resident, Kabul, July 2, 2003.

center [at the top of Afshar mountain] and it was on fire. The base was on fire. There was a lot of artillery landing nearby."[173]

One resident, a Tajik man who lived in Afshar, said that the constant firing of shells and rockets kept many residents inside: "Before the invasion, there was no announcement or effort to make people leave, or evacuate. No one knew what was happening, everyone was a prisoner in their home."[174] The man described seeing a neighbor hit by shrapnel on or about February 7:

> Mir Yaqub, a neighbor of mine just next to me, in the house below, a rocket hit his house and he was killed. This was about four days before the main attack started. After the rocket hit, I looked out this little space, between the bags of dirt we had laid in the windows. I looked out and down into his yard, and I saw that he had been injured, and was lying on the ground. Members of his family picked him up . . . to take him to the hospital, but he died [there], and they brought him back and buried him on the mountain.[175]

The Ground Attack

The Afshar operation started in earnest in the early hours of February 11, 1993. Jamiat forces (with Harakat's agreement to allow it) seized the top of Afshar mountain itself. Ittihad and Jamiat positions then launched a massive barrage of rockets and artillery at the entire area around the foot of the mountain—both the Wahdat positions along the main road south of Afshar and the neighborhood to the north. Much of the barrage hit civilian homes in Afshar area through the morning.[176] As the morning continued,

---

[173] Human Rights Watch interview with with J.L.S., Afshar resident, Kabul, July 6, 2003.

[174] Human Rights Watch interview with A.S.F., Tajik man from Afshar, Kabul, July 2, 2003. The resident described the barrage in detail: "The rockets were coming from different directions. The path could be seen in the earth, the scratch into the earth. There were different sounds: sometimes a humming sound, sometimes a fast flapping sound, for about two or three seconds before the explosion. Before the shells there would be a deep whistling noise."

[175] Human Rights Watch interview with A.S.F., Tajik man from Afshar, Kabul, July 2, 2003.

[176] A resident told Human Rights Watch about how ordinance continued to fall into civilian homes: "That day, it was a terrible day. Sakr rockets were hitting altogether, in dozens. One rocket hit near my house and a person died nearby. Two houses above ours, two other people were killed. One explosion happened in the next house above ours, and six or seven people were killed." Human Rights Watch interview with L.M., Afshar resident, Kabul, July 12, 2003.

Wahdat troops fled south, away from Afshar. Ittihad and Jamiat forces began to enter the area.[177]

L.S., an Afshar resident, told Human Rights Watch how the morning unfolded:

> It was five o' clock in the morning. There were rockets firing and artillery. . . . At first, people thought: "It is fighting between the mujahedin." I myself thought this, and I didn't worry so much. I thought that they were fighting amongst themselves—Rabbani, Wahdat—and that civilians would face no harm. But there was a lot of rocketing. Then around ten a.m. we saw the first troops come from the west, into Afshar. . . . We stayed indoors.[178]

A.L.S., another resident who was a boy when the attack occurred, said that many families started to flee as the morning progressed, including his own:

> It was terrible. There were rockets, explosions. . . . I saw a rocket hit a neighbor's house. His son was killed. There was blood pouring out of him. I saw that. . . . The [ground] attack started sometime later. Our family left [then]. When we went, we saw a lot of dead bodies on the street: people who had been killed.[179]

Many families tried to go east, towards the Hotel Intercontinental and into the Timani neighborhood beyond, where many people later took refuge.

---

[177] Human Rights Watch telephone interview with John Jennings, Associated Press correspondent in Kabul 1992-1993, April 10, 2004 (describing events on Thursday morning); Human Rights Watch interview with Q.E.K., former political official in Wahdat who observed attack from west Kabul, Kabul, July 15, 2003. J.L.S., a resident quoted above who was higher up on the mountain, said he and some of his neighbors saw troops entering Afshar in the morning, and they took refuge in a small cave in the side of the mountain: "After that, we didn't move. We stayed where we were until late at night. The troops were going among the houses, we could see. . . ." Human Rights Watch interview with J.L.S., Afshar resident, Kabul, July 6, 2003.

[178] Human Rights Watch interview with L.S., Afshar resident, Kabul, July 4, 2003.

[179] Human Rights Watch interview with A.L.S., Afshar resident, Kabul, July 6, 2003.

A resident, Q.L.N., described the scene of fleeing residents: "A number of families were fleeing. One family was holding a dead child, wouldn't let it go. One young girl had lost her family; she was wounded, dying on the ground."[180]

Ittihad troops were now arresting Hazara men: numerous residents interviewed by Human Rights Watch described Ittihad troops stopping Hazara men and separating them from their families.[181] The troops were also killing unarmed civilians. F.A., a woman from Afshar, told Human Rights Watch about how both her husband and son were killed by Ittihad troops the first day of the attack:

> As we were leaving [to flee Afshar], three of Sayyaf's gunmen came up to our house. My husband, my son, and us women. Just as we opened our door, they were there. They came in, and without exchanging a single word, they aimed their guns at my husband and my son and they shot both of them, right in front of our eyes. . . . We were hitting our heads and sobbing and throwing ourselves on our men. The troops said that if we didn't stop screaming they would throw grenades at us and kill us. . . .[182]

(The woman later fled east with another family to Taimani, a predominately ethnic Ismaili neighborhood where many Afshar residents took refuge during the attack.[183])

Another woman, F.W., said she had to leave her wounded husband behind as she fled:

> That first day, a rocket hit our house. My husband was wounded in the foot. He was bleeding. . . . People were rushing around: men, women, children, all fleeing their houses, going toward the Intercontinental Hotel. I told my husband, "Everyone is leaving, fleeing, no one is left." And I said that we should go. But he said, "I can't move. I can't go

---

[180] Human Rights Watch interview with Q.L.N., Afshar resident, Kabul, July 23, 2003.

[181] Human Rights Watch interview with F.W., woman in Afshar, Kabul, July 2, 2003; Human Rights Watch interview with Y.B.K., July 11, 2003; Human Rights Watch interview with L.M., July 12, 2003; Human Rights Watch interview with L.S., July 4, 2003.

[182] Human Rights Watch interview with F.A., woman from Afshar, Kabul, July 6, 2003.

[183] Ibid. Another Afshar woman, F.W., explained: "The Ismaili people helped us when we got past that area—in their mosque. The leaders of the Ismaili people divided us up, to live with Ismaili people, and they ordered the Ismaili people to be hospitable to us, and they were." Human Rights Watch interview with F.W., woman in Afshar, Kabul, July 2, 2003.

with you. Leave me here, and flee." And he told me to take the eldest daughter, and that taking her away was the most important thing. . . .

We went out [of the house], but I couldn't go. I couldn't leave him there—my husband. I had to go back. So I went back, and I told him that I wanted him to come with us, and that I would help him walk. . . . So then we went, I was helping him, he had his arm around my shoulder. I was also carrying my three-month-old son, and my eldest daughter was holding my three-year-old. We got as far as the water canal [about 80 meters away].

At that moment, some gunmen came up to us, Mullah Ezatullah's men. The commander said, "Qalfak Chapat." [A derogatory term for Hazaras referring to their facial features.] "I'm one of Ezatullah's men, and I've been ordered to seize this area. I'll teach you a lesson you'll never forget, for all of history." He was a fat strong man, in plain Afghan clothes. But they didn't do anything to us. They said, "We can reach you anywhere you go, we are everywhere, we control everything." And they moved on.

So we were very scared. My husband said he could not go on. So we went back to our house. He made us leave, he insisted that I take our daughter, and so we went. We went [past] the Intercontinental . . . and we went to the Ismaili people [in Taimani], who helped us.

A few days later, a neighbor came to us, a Tajik who knew what was going on. He told us that Afshar was destroyed, my house was burned, and my husband was killed. . . .[184]

The woman returned to the house over a year later: "When we entered the house, we found only a skull, and four big bones, on the ground. There was nothing else. A neighbor, who knew Sayyaf's people and had seen more of what happened, told me that my husband was shot with many bullets and killed."[185]

---

[184] Human Rights Watch interview with F.W., woman in Afshar, Kabul, July 2, 2003.

[185] Ibid.

Another resident, R.J.G., said that he witnessed rockets fired into crowds of fleeing civilians off the top of Afshar mountain on the afternoon of February 11:

> Jamiat took the top of the mountain. Around five in the afternoon, they started firing rockets from the top of the mountain, down into this area. They killed people right here on this street. People were rushing out of Afshar. They were rushing down this street here [the main street running north south through the eastern part of Afshar]. The street was filled with people, running away from Afshar. . . . My house is right there, at the top of the street. . . . Massoud's forces were shooting at them. . . . They were firing into this street. Three times the street was hit. Seventeen people were killed—there were seventeen bodies lying in the street—we counted. The corpses were lying here in the streets. . . . Clearly they were civilians. Yes, it was clear: they had burqas, there were children. It was clear they were civilians.[186]

Another resident, L.M., was almost killed by a rocket the next day:

> As we were walking up towards our compound, a shell or a rocket hit right in front of my compound. I was walking with my two neighbors, both of them were hit. One was killed instantly. A piece of the rocket went into his eye, and out the back of his head. He died. And the other person was hit in the knee, and he was injured, and he fell down. We were about fifty meters from where the explosion was. . . . I was not wounded. It was a miracle.[187]

Notably, this incident, which took place in a residential area, occurred after Wahdat forces had left the nearby headquarters, suggesting that whatever force fired the rocket was either intentionally or recklessly targeting civilians.

Y.B.K., a Hazara Afshar resident who was a boy at the time, said he was arrested in his house by troops he believed were Pashtun—likely Ittihad—and taken to the Academy of Social Science. He said he saw scores of dead civilians on the way.[188]

---

[186] Human Rights Watch interview with R.J.G., Afshar resident, Kabul, July 6, 2003.

[187] Human Rights Watch interview with L.M., Afshar resident, Kabul, July 12, 2003.

[188] This account is taken from a Human Rights Watch interview with Y.B.K., former resident of Afshar as a young boy, July 11, 2003.

I saw some Paghmani people [i.e., Ittihad], searching house by house. I fled into my house. This commander, Hasan Yaldar [the witness said he learned the name of the commander from his neighbor, mentioned below], came into our house, with seven or eight gunmen. . . . They grabbed me and took me with them. I was afraid. . . . Hasan Yaldar pushed me down to the ground, and he kneeled on my chest, pulled out his bayonet, and pushed it into [against] my throat. —"Where are the guns?" he yelled at me. —"I don't know anything, I swear to God," I said. But he hit me with a strong slap. And he was yelling at me. I was crying and crying. I was so afraid. Then, the other gunmen told him to release him, and he did, and they started to beat me, kicking me, punching me, and hitting me with their guns. I had cuts all over my body. I was hurt badly.

My neighbor, a Panshiri [Tajik], came up and he tried to stop them. He said to Hasan Yaldar, "He's just a child!" And he said to them that when Wahdat was in power, my family had protected them [as Tajiks] as much as possible, and that he had to protect me. But they took me away. They made me walk toward the Academy of Social Science.

On the way, I saw fifty or sixty corpses all over the roads. Some were shot. Some were cut up, limbs severed. There was a lot of blood on the ground. It was a shocking scene. It stuck in my mind how awful it was. . . . Some of them were shot. I saw some bodies, their stomachs had been cut open. Others had been hit in explosions, in rockets, and were burned. . . . I think that most were killed by gunmen. . . .

My neighbor was following us, begging them to release me. He was trying to convince them, saying I was just a child, and asking them again and again. Finally, I think he talked to a higher commander, who told Hasan Yaldar to release me. Finally, they released me, and my neighbor grabbed my hand, and took me back to my house, to my mother. We were in a panic. . . .[189]

---

[189] Human Rights Watch interview with Y.B.K., former resident of Afshar as a young boy, July 11, 2003.

F.W., quoted above, who fled during the fighting east toward the Hotel Intercontinental, said that some troops were stopping civilians and killing some of them at the side of the road, although at least one commander attempted to stop abuses:

> While we were fleeing, toward the Intercontinental, the troops were stopping civilians, and killing them. One of the commanders said to the troops, "Stop bothering these people. We are fighting with gunmen, not children and wives." But some others disagreed with him, and said, "No, on the battlefield, everyone is an enemy. Everyone who helps the enemy is an enemy."[190]

Some residents said that Jamiat troops stopped Hazaras as well, and arrested them. Q.L.N told Human Rights Watch that he saw Jamiat troops stopping Hazara civilians at a post at Bagh Bala: "Qari Moheb, the Jamiat commander, stopped me. . . . They took my watch, my clothes. . . . There were two wounded people in the car with me, Hazara. They [the Jamiat troops] just said 'You're Hazara, you must come with us.'"[191] Q.L.N. said he was able to be released because another Jamiat commander there knew him. "The others were taken," he said.

On February 12, as more Ittihad troops fanned through the neighborhood, residents continued to flee. According to numerous residents interviewed, Ittihad troops were still stopping Hazara families, separating men from their families and arresting them, and sometimes beating or killing them.

L.M., an Ismaili, told Human Rights Watch that Ittihad troops (after they robbed his store nearby) asked him which houses were inhabited by Hazaras: "'Where are the Hazaras?' they said. I said, 'I don't know, we all live in different houses, I don't know.'"[192] A short-time later, as troops continued to move through Afshar, some Hazara neighbors came to L.M.'s house asking him for help: "[T]hese two Hazara guys came into my house, some neighbors, and they said, 'We live nearby. We know that you

---

[190] Human Rights Watch interview with F.W., woman in Afshar, Kabul, July 2, 2003.

[191] Human Rights Watch interview with Q.L.N., Afshar resident, Kabul, July 23, 2003.

[192] Human Rights Watch interview with L.M., Afshar resident, Kabul, July 12, 2003.

are a good person. Please help us, they are looking for us.'"[193]   L.M. said that family members later escorted the two men out of Afshar.[194]

As he fled later, L.M. saw Ittihad troops beating a Hazara teenager at a checkpost:

> [H]e was the son of the servant at the mosque. He was behind us [as we left Afshar]. The gunmen stopped him, and started to beat him. I turned around, and I said, "Stop, he is the son of the servant at the mosque. He's not a fighter." But they pulled him off and took him away somewhere. Three days later, when I came back, I saw his corpse behind the wall of the Academy of Social Science. I saw two corpses; his was one of them.[195]

L.S., a Hazara man quoted above, described what he saw and experienced:[196]

> When I looked into the street, I saw a lot of people, men, women, and children running down the hill, escaping. . . . We decided to leave. . . . I got outside of my house, with my wife and children, and we started to flee. Along the way, we came upon gunmen, who were arresting people. They were stopping the families, and separating the men from the families. There were about seven or eight gunmen. They saw us, and some of them came up to us and they separated me from my family. . . .

L.S. said that he saw thirty to forty other Hazara men and boys lined up against a wall, guarded by Ittihad troops:

> The gunmen were tying people up and putting them against the wall. Women were crying, or they were running away. They were very afraid.

---

[193] Ibid.

[194] Ibid. "I told them to go upstairs, and I told my family to make them some tea. But they said, "No, you are very kind, but we have not come for tea. We are in danger, and we need to do something." We agreed. We had to leave. So I took all my family, and my neighbor's family, and these two Hazaras, and we left. We went down to the road, and we hired a car we found somehow, nearby, and moved towards Kha Khana."

[195] Human Rights Watch interview with L.M., Afshar resident, Kabul, July 12, 2003.

[196] The following quotes are taken from a Human Rights Watch interview with L.S., July 4, 2003.

The soldiers saw us and came over to us. I know who the commander was: Shir Agha Zarshakh. It was one of Sayyaf's commanders.

According to L.S., Shir Agha Zarshakh addressed him specifically:

He said, "Hey, Hazara: this is your graveyard. Where are you going?"

I said, "I am an ordinary person. I have no involvement with political parties or fighting. I live here with my family."

He said, "Whether you are a civilian or not a civilian, you are Hazara." And immediately the soldiers started beating me with the butts of their guns. My seven-year old son rushed away from my wife towards me, to help me, but one of the gunmen hit him hard with a gun, and knocked him down to the ground. Then the gunman took the bayonet off his gun, and put it up to my boy's throat, like to cut off his head. I started shrieking, and the women started shrieking, and my wife and some other women threw themselves on top of the boy. The soldier moved back, toward me. I signaled with my hand to my wife to leave, to go. Then the women rushed off with the boy.

L.S. said he saw two women killed by the same set of troops:

At this time, they killed some women also. . . . This is how it happened: Najaf Karbalie [one who has made a pilgrimage to Karbala], an old man, had come out of his house, and they had separated him from his family to arrest him. As this happened, his wife came to him and grabbed him and was pulling on him, saying, "Please, leave him, he is old. Leave him." But the gunmen did not let go of him.

Karbalie said to the gunmen, "Well, we thought you were Muslim. If we had known that you would behave like this, you would never have succeeded in capturing Afshar." And the gunmen started beating him. They were also beating someone else, next to him. Karbalie's wife and another woman threw themselves on them, their husbands, and were yelling at the troops, insulting them. The troops grabbed the one woman, and then the other, pushed them off the men, and then threw them on the ground and killed them.

They took their guns, with the bayonets, and stabbed the women as they lay on the ground, stabbed them many times over, at least ten times. [Motions like he is holding a gun with a bayonet, stabbing it down into the ground.] We saw all of this.

After, the women were lying on the ground. They were shaking at first; their feet were twitching. They were dead. The two men, both of them, fainted. They were unconscious. The women were about thirty-five, or forty. I think that one of them was pregnant. She looked pregnant. . . .

J.L.S., quoted above, a physically disabled Hazara man in Afshar who was detained in a house by Ittihad troops on February 12, told Human Rights Watch that troops beat him: "They beat me, really badly. I am a lame person [disabled]. I said [to them], 'I am just a lame man, I can hardly walk.'"[197] J.L.S. also said the troops harassed his female relatives:

They went to the women in my family, and they started to grab them, and pull at their chador [to remove it]. I threw myself on the legs of the troops, and said, "How dare you search these women?" This one troop I grabbed, he took his gun and pointed it down at me [to shoot me], but one of the women grabbed the butt of the gun before it fired, and the shot went into the ground. The women cried, "Please, give us mercy, he is just a lame man." And they let us go. They said, "We'll come back for you later."

Y.B.K., quoted above, said that Ittihad troops started searching houses, apparently to look for weapons but also to harass Hazara civilians. He described seeing one of his neighbors being harassed, a 70-year-old man:

They said, "Hey, old man, where are your guns?" The old man said, "I don't have anything, I don't have any guns." But the troops knocked him down and punched him. They took him by the ankles and held him upside down into the well [hanging into the well], and yelled at him: "Where are the guns?" But he yelled out, "My dear son, have mercy on me! I don't have any guns!" They pulled him up again, and they threw him on the ground. . . .[198]

---

[197] Human Rights Watch interview with J.L.S., Afshar resident, Kabul, July 6, 2003.

[198] Human Rights Watch interview with Y.B.K., former resident of Afshar, July 11, 2003.

R.J.G., quoted above, fled Afshar with his family early on the morning of February 12. He said that Jamiat forces near the Hotel Intercontinental stopped his family and told them that the "fighting was over" and told them return to Afshar. R.J.G. and his family returned. "But when we got back, we could see that Sayyaf's forces were there—and that there were Kandaharis among them, and that they were looting." He fled once again: "We saw that there was no security, so we left again. There were many, many corpses [on the roads]."[199] As he left his house for the second time, R.J.G. said he saw Ittihad troops randomly kill a Hazara boy who was passing a nearby checkpost on the way out of Afshar:

> I saw Sayyaf's troops kill this guy on the street here, a Hazara, about 16 years old. I saw from my house. There were these gunmen posted here, and this guy was passing on his way down the road. The gunmen, they were Pashtuns. They didn't do anything to the boy as he went by, and the boy passed. After he passed, they shot him in the back, two of them I think, and he was killed. . . .[200]

Evidence of Mutilations, and Cases of Looting and Forced Labor

Ittihad forces compelled persons they had taken into custody to bury the dead, and those who did so say they saw evidence of torture and mutilation of corpses. Ittihad forces were also reported to have forced captured civilians to assist them in looting property and otherwise take part in forced labor.

L.S., quoted above, told Human Rights Watch that after he was arrested on February 12, Ittihad gunmen forced him to bury corpses and load trucks with stolen goods:

> [After we were arrested,] three trucks arrived. Since my home was closest, they made us go into that house, to take out the property. They made us go in and carry all my property to the truck. We loaded property from many houses. . . .[201]

---

[199] Human Rights Watch interview with R.J.G., Afshar resident, Kabul, July 6, 2003. Another resident complained that troops made no efforts help fleeing civilians: "Shura-e Nazar didn't say anything to us about whether to stay or go. I didn't know the corridor out [where it was safe to flee to], it was chaos." Human Rights Watch interview with A.Q.L., Afshar resident, July 21, 2003.

[200] Human Rights Watch interview with R.J.G., July 6, 2003.

[201] Human Rights Watch interview with L.S., Afshar resident, Kabul, July 4, 2003.

L.S. said that he and other detainees were then taken to the campus of the Polytechnic University nearby, where they were tied up. L.S. said that Ittihad troops beat them once they were tied up, kicking them and hitting them with their guns.[202]

Abdul Rabb al-Rasul Sayyaf, the leader of the Ittihad faction, speaking on television during Afghanistan's constitutional loya jirga, December 2003. Several delegates to the 2003 loya jirga condemned Sayyaf and other commanders for their involvement in war crimes and human rights abuses in Kabul in the early 1990s.
© 2003 Human Rights Watch

The men were later untied, said L.S., and deployed to pick up dead civilians and bury them. "They said, 'Go and collect your corpses in Afshar, go collect your dead.' So we went out, with them guarding us."[203]

> The first person we found was Faizal Ahmed, an old man. He was decapitated. One of his arms was cut off and one of his legs. And his penis was cut off, and his penis was put in his mouth.

---

[202] Human Rights Watch interview with L.S., July 4, 2003.

[203] Ibid.

Then we collected three other corpses, near Balki's shrine, and four others from the street between the Academy of Social Science and the police academy. We buried all of these eight across from the Polytechnic mosque, in the potato field there.

Then they separated us, the older men from the young men. [The witness is an older man.] They took us to Qala Hazrat Sayeed and to Qala Qorna [Old Mosque]. The old to the old: I was in the Old Mosque. They made us put property from these areas into trucks. We loaded the property, and they took all the property off to Paghman. These people were from Paghman. They drove the trucks off to the west, toward Paghman.

As they were looting, they were saying, "You Hazaras were asking to be kings,[204] but you don't deserve these things. We deserve these things."

Until eight p.m. it was our duty to load property from these houses in Afshar into the trucks. We had nothing to eat. When we asked for water, they were saying to us, "You should drink poison." We were drinking water from the wells in some of the houses, as we were taking the property. Almost forty trucks were loaded, I think.[205]

The Ittihad troops, L.S. said, then took L.S. back to the Old Mosque, where he and other prisoners were tied up and kept for the night. "Some people slept," he said. "Most did not. We feared death."[206] The next morning they buried more corpses, said L.S., although later in the day Ittihad troops made them load more trucks and told them to stop trying to pick up the dead:

From seven to ten a.m., we found eleven corpses. . . . We found one seven-year-old boy, he was decapitated. His head was nearby, it had been cut off, from behind: you could see from the head that they cut from the back, and that the skin had been torn off from the front of his neck, not cut. We found a woman in the same house, dead. She was

---

[204] This is a possible reference to the Wahdat party's demands in December 1992 that it be given a larger share of posts in the interim government.

[205] Human Rights Watch interview with L.S., July 4, 2003.

[206] Ibid.

holding a copy of the Koran in her arms, embracing it. Then we found the two women who I told you about before, who had been stabbed. We found seven other bodies, in the streets. Men. They had been shot. Three of them were shot in the head. We buried them behind Balki mosque, on the east side. . . . Later, we loaded more trucks: at around two p.m., we went to Cotton Textile Street, and Shir Ali Street, and took the property out of those houses. In a house on Cotton Textile Street, we saw a man, Haji Hasan: his head was cut off, and his feet, and his hands. There was nowhere to bury him, and no time: they were not letting us bury the corpses. So we put him into the well there. It would be better for him than to be eaten by dogs. . . .

The Ittihad troops apparently wanted to leave some evidence of their crimes—to terrorize the local population:

Then we went on to Shir Ali street. There, there was a woman who was shot. She had been the wife of the servant in the mosque there. We wanted to bury her, but they didn't let us. They said, "Let her lie here. Let the other people learn from this, and fear us."

On Jaghori Street, there was a guy there, Hussein Ali, he was about eighteen. He had been shot. They did not let us bury him either. "There are many others like him, you can't spend all your time burying people." [They said.] "There are others who will be eaten by dogs, let him be eaten too." These all were Shir Agha Zarshakh's men. He was with us the whole time.[207]

L.S. said he escaped from custody the second night after he was arrested. He says that the Ittihad men guarding them at the Old Mosque left them alone in the evening:

I and an old man and his nephew threw ourselves out of a window there. We crept up Afshar Mountain, and got to the water canal. There, we crawled all night, on our knees and elbows, across the hill, in the canal, to the northeast. All the skin was worn off our elbows. We moved on, toward the center of the city, and joined the other Afshari people at the Qahraman Karbala Mosque [in Taimani]. . . . Of the forty other people who were imprisoned with me, we never heard of them

---

[207] Ibid.

again, or found them. We have talked to their families: none of them was ever returned, and no one ever saw them again.[208]

A.Q.L., another Hazara man who was arrested during the operation, told Human Rights Watch that he was also forced to help Ittihad troops loot homes:

> Four armed men from Sayyaf's forces came. It was around 10 a.m. I begged for mercy, saying, "We are commoners." They said: "You are Hazara, you work for Mazari." They beat me up. . . . Sayyaf's men forced me to carry the loot. . . .[209]

Y.B.K., also quoted above, said that he saw Ittihad troops forcing residents to carry looted goods: "The troops were making [people who they arrested] drag precious things with them, like they were porters. They were carrying what the troops looted, behind them."[210] He saw civilians forced to "drag the corpses out on to the street."[211] He also said his own home was looted: "They took everything valuable. What they couldn't take, they broke into pieces—for instance, the refrigerators."[212]

Soldiers involved in looting did so openly, apparently unconcerned that their superiors would try to stop them:

> At around twelve that day I heard some drums. I was amazed. Who would be having a wedding in the middle of this massacre? I looked outside and saw the troops walking by, playing on drums, laughing. They had some porters with them, carrying some televisions and radios.[213]

---

[208] Human Rights Watch interview with L.S., Afshar resident, Kabul, July 4, 2003.

[209] Human Rights Watch interview with A.Q.L., Afshar resident, July 21, 2003.

[210] Human Rights Watch interview with Y.B.K., former resident of Afshar as a young boy, July 11, 2003.

[211] Ibid.

[212] Ibid.

[213] Ibid.

L.M., the Ismaili man quoted above, was also detained and forced to work, after he returned to Afshar to look for his son, who had gone back to get some of his belongings and (as L.M. later learned) was detained as well.[214]

> I saw many corpses on the road. . . . Many had been shot, or stabbed. I went to my home. Everything was stolen. There was nothing there. They had taken all the valuable things, and what was left, too big to take, had been broken, and shot with bullets, like the refrigerator.[215]

L.M. said he could not find his son, and he went to a nearby mosque to pray:

> I was really upset, and feeling very sad and broken. I went to the shrine, and I prayed there. When I finished praying, I stood up, and some gunmen saw me. They called me over, and they said, "Old man! Who are you?" I said, "I am an inhabitant of this area." And they said, "Oh yes, we know you. You have two guns. Give them to us." I said, "Believe me, I swear to God, I am only a shopkeeper." They said, "No, you are a fighter, give us the guns." I said again, "I don't have any." But they started to beat me. They all beat me, all of them. I fell to the ground, my eyes were hurt, they turned black and blue later. My head was full of bumps. After they beat me, they made me stand up, and they ordered me to walk towards the north of Afshar, with them. As we went, they entered into houses, to search, or to shoot people. They were laughing, enjoying themselves.

L.M. said that the troops took him into a small cemetery, where he says he saw the corpses of about eleven boys:

> They made me walk up and stand next to those corpses. They said to me, "Give us the guns, or you will face the same fate as these eleven boys." They were all around me, pointing their guns. They ordered me to sit down on the ground. The commander said, "I'll count to three, and you have to confess."

---

[214] Human Rights Watch interview with L.M., Afshar resident, Kabul, July 12, 2003.

[215] Ibid.

I said, "I am a Muslim, let me pray, and then kill me." They told me: "You're dirty, you're not a Muslim—you're Shi'a."

So then I just started praying, with my mouth [i.e., not out loud]. They counted, "One. . . Two . . . Three," and then they fired, right in front of me, so that the dirt on the ground sprayed up into my face. . . . It was on automatic.

"O.K.," they said. "He won't confess. He will die digging holes for us in Paghman. There is no need to kill him." So then they took me away.

A more senior commander then appeared and asked the other troops who L.M. was:

They said, "We have arrested him. He has two guns, and he won't give them to us." The man said, "Shoot him. Kill him. Don't waste your time. And put his corpse with the others." And he pointed towards the cemetery.

But the troops apparently had other ideas. L.M. says they took him to a nearby compound, Qala Said, where there was a *tokia khana*, a Shi'a prayer hall, and made him carry out belongings from it: "They made me go in and carry out many valuable things, everything. They sent for a truck, to load things into."

Then the troops put L.M. in a car and drove west with him, toward Paghman.

When we got to the Qargha, they stopped. There was a house there. We went into that house, and there they divided up all the property. I carried the property into the house. I saw them divide it. The commander got two shares, and the soldiers got one share.

L.M. spent the night there, sleeping on the ground at the Qargha base. The troops, who seem to have taken an inexplicable liking to L.M., drove him back into Kabul the next morning and released him.

A.Q.L., quoted earlier, said that after he was forced to help loot homes in Afshar, Ittihad troops took him with them back to Paghman and made him build fortifications.[216]

---

[216] Human Rights Watch interview with A.Q.L., Afshar resident, July 21, 2003.

A.Q.L. says he was then kept there, essentially as a slave, for the next three years, working on a base controlled by Zalmay Tofan, one of Sayyaf's main commanders.

> They took me to Khandaq Tarik in Kampani, to Zalmay Tofan's base. . . . They threw us in a container. There were forty prisoners there, Hazaras, in that one container. Every day they gave us one piece of bread and slapped us. By day we worked, by night we were put in the container. It was very cold; there was no sleep. I stayed there for forty days. Then they transferred us to Badam Ghol in Paghman. . . . There were twelve of us [there]. We went to a mountain between Maidanshah [district west of Kabul] and Paghman. There were four posts on that mountain. . . . I built these posts; I carried all the food and water there.

> [When asked how he knew the commander's name:] The men there told us "We are Zalmay's men." Conditions were very bad. . . . At dinner, they manacled us with chains on the legs, two of us to a chain. . . . We stayed in a room, about three by four meters. . . We never received anything from Sayyaf and Tofan. But after Sakhi came [another commander], he at least loosed our manacles at night, our food improved. I stayed there for three years. I had no news from my family. Out of the twelve [prisoners], one died due to disease. We couldn't escape, because if one escaped the rest were under pressure. . . . I saw Zalmay Tofan up close personally once; it was in the second year I was up there.[217]

A.Q.L. says he was released in 1996, as the Taliban seized control of the area and Ittihad troops fled north. He then set off to find his family:

> It took me eleven days to walk to Kabul. It was snowy, it was winter. . . [A] car came, he agreed to give us a ride. . . .

> [When] I saw my face in the [car] mirror, I was shocked. The driver paid for the barber, for our shoes and clothes. I was dropped in Taimani. It was quiet, I didn't know anyone anymore. I found someone I knew; he said your family is in Karte Seh, so I went there.

> [Witness was quite distressed, but refused to stop interview.]

---

[217] Ibid.

My wife didn't recognize me, only after a few minutes.[218]

Both A.Q.L. and L.M. (quoted earlier) told Human Rights Watch that their sons were also arrested by Ittihad. A.Q.L. said his son was only eight years old when he was taken, and was kept for over three years: "After Sayyaf's forces were defeated by the Taliban [in 1996], he was kept imprisoned by the Taliban. . . . I paid a lot of money to the Taliban and then he was released."[219] Human Rights Watch has documented that many young boys were and are still held by commanders for the purposes of sexual abuse.[220] A.Q.L. did not allow Human Rights Watch to interview his son: "It is not good to remind the child from his bitter memories in the past."[221]

L.M.'s son was 16 when he was arrested. L.M. managed to have him released after about two months, when he learned that he was being held at Bagh-e Daoud, in Paghman, by a commander under Mullah Ezatullah, named Masjida:

> I went to Bagh-e Daoud, to the post there. . . . I eventually got a meeting with a commander named Ghafar, who was under Mullah Ezat, and he ordered Masjida to release my son. And so Masjida released him to me. I took him with me from that compound and brought him home.[222]

L.M.'s son, who was held for about two months, became mentally ill soon after his release. Said L.M.: "For a month or so, my son was alright, he was quiet, depressed, but

---

[218] Ibid.

[219] Human Rights Watch interview with A.Q.L., Afshar resident, July 21, 2003.

[220] See Human Rights Watch, *"Killing You is a Very Easy Thing For Us": Human Rights Abuses in Southeast Afghanistan*, A Human Rights Watch Short Report, vol. 15, no. 5 (C), July 2003, available at http://www.hrw.org/reports/2003/afghanistan0703/, section III, subsection entitled "Rape of Boys"; Human Rights Watch, *"All Our Hopes are Crushed": Violence and Repression in Western Afghanistan*, A Human Rights Watch Short Report, vol. 14, no. 7(C), October 2002, available at http://hrw.org/reports/2002/afghan3/herat1002-06.htm#P997_155129, section IV entitled "Torture and Arbitrary Arrests"; Human Rights Watch, "On the Precipice: Insecurity in Northern Afghanistan," A Human Rights Watch Briefing Paper, June 2002, available at http://www.hrw.org/backgrounder/asia/afghanistan/afghan-bck-04.htm, section IV entitled "Continued abuses against Pashtuns in Faryab."

[221] Human Rights Watch interview with A.Q.L., Afshar resident, July 21, 2003.

[222] Human Rights Watch interview with L.M., Afshar resident, Kabul, July 12, 2003.

more or less he was of sound mind. Now he is insane."[223] Human Rights Watch researchers observed L.M.'s son in 2003, in a semi-catatonic state. According to his family, he no longer communicates with other people, and spends his days sleeping or staring into space, sometimes muttering or laughing. L.M. described what his son told him before his mental health problems set in:

> [Before the mental health problems,] I asked about what had happened to him. He wouldn't talk so much about it. But he said this: he said he tried to escape from that compound once. He said he had tried to run away, but that they had fired guns at him. He said that that had really shocked him. . . . There were five or six other prisoners who were held with my son. He told me that. . . . They were made to work, my son said. He said they did work for the commanders and troops, washing their clothes, chopping wood, and that sort of thing.[224]

As detailed in earlier sections, Ittihad was not the only faction implicated in abductions. The Afshar campaign also exposed further Wahdat abuses: An Ittihad soldier who fought in the Afshar campaign told Human Rights Watch that after his troops seized the Academy of Social Science from Wahdat, they found several women there who said they had been raped by Wahdat. They also found a small pile of corpses of women prisoners. In another room, they found another pile of dead men and approximately twenty-five male prisoners: "They were all completely insane—from being tortured. They were completely, completely insane.[225] The man said he was unable to stay longer to get a more detailed look: "I ran away. Because of the smell. It was disgusting."[226]

The effects of the Afshar campaign

It is impossible to know for certain how many civilians were killed during the Afshar campaign, and how many were abducted and never released. After the Rabbani government came under strong pressure from Shi'a community leaders in the summer of 1993, they assigned a commission to catalog the destruction, for the purposes of paying out some form of compensation. The commission was comprised of civilians appointed by Wahdat and Harakat leaders, and they received complaints from families of approximately 800 arrests during the operation, mostly males between the ages of ten

---

[223] Ibid.

[224] Ibid.

[225] Human Rights Watch interview with K.M.B., former combatant who served under Ittihad forces, Kabul, July 4, 2003.

[226] Ibid.

and thirty-five, with a small number of younger children and older men. According to officials, the final documents produced by this commission were destroyed after the Taliban captured Kabul in 1996.[227]

Officials with the commission said that approximately eighty to two hundred persons were later released, and that ransoms were paid to Ittihad commanders holding them to secure their release, but that approximately 700-750 persons were never returned, and were presumably killed or died in captivity.[228] The commission said it documented that approximately 70 to 80 people were also killed in the streets in Afshar, a figure which is consistent with the testimony in this report. The same official said that the commission received information that many women were abducted during the operation, but said that few families would report it:

> People were feeling so much shame: no one was reporting that the females were taken. [It was] because of the dishonor, and shame, families would report that the women were killed. [T]he men were reported kidnapped, and the women were reported killed [but] there is no doubt that women were kidnapped.[229]

The commission estimated that approximately 5,000 houses were looted in the Afshar area during and after the operation, a figure which is not inconsistent with the accounts and information received by Human Rights Watch.[230]

The larger import of the campaign was felt through Kabul. Many Kabulis viewed Afshar as a milestone in the post-communist era, a moment when they realized the real ethnic tensions underlying the fighting in Kabul and the extent to which different mujahedin factions—who had mainly fought the Soviet regime for so long—were now prepared to

---

[227] Human Rights Watch interview with P.G., member of 1993 commission appointed to estimate civilian damage during the Afshar campaign, Kabul, July 4, 2003; Human Rights Watch interview with Q.E.K., former Wahdat official in 1993 commission appointed to estimate civilian damage during the Afshar campaign, Kabul, July 15, 2003.

[228] Human Rights Watch interview with P.G., July 4, 2003 and Human Rights Watch interview with Q.E.K., July 15, 2003.

[229] Human Rights Watch interview with P.G., July 4, 2003.

[230] A Shura-e Nazar official also told Human Rights Watch that the government received numerous complaints that Jamiat forces looted buildings around the Silo south of Afshar and in areas to the east of the Afshar neighborhood. Human Rights Watch interview with R.D., former official in the interim government 1992-1995, Kabul, July 16, 2003.

kill fellow Afghans. Much of the rest of the civil war, even into the Taliban period, was almost wholly defined in terms of ethnic and religious tensions between the different factions, stemming from perceived injustices which occurred in the first year of post-communist rule, the Afghan year 1371, which ended with the Afshar incident.

After Afshar

The Afshar campaign and the surrounding violence were ended by a short-lived peace agreement fashioned in late February 1993. (Hamid Gul, the former head of Pakistan's Inter-Services Intelligence, or ISI, flew into Kabul in February and took part in negotiations.) Hekmatyar was granted a position in the Rabbani government as prime minister, but would not enter the city to take up his post. There were a few weeks of relative calm, but the peace did not last. By late March, Hezb-e Islami forces were again attacking Jamiat and Ittihad positions in the city. Violence continued in the city throughout the year. By the end of 1993, Junbish switched sides and join Hekmatyar's forces, launching a new chapter of violence in the city. January 1994 was marked by huge battles in east Kabul, more shelling, and more civilian deaths. Violence continued through 1994 into 1995, at which point the Taliban began its attacks on Kabul, which were also marked by grave violations and abuses.

Civilians fleeing Kabul, March 5, 1993. Over a half million people were displaced by fighting in Kabul in 1992-1993. © 1993 Robert Nickelsberg

THE BATTLE FOR KABUL

This report, which focuses on the first year of the post-Najibullah government, does not cover events after March 1993. But Human Rights Watch has gathered large amounts of information on further abuses in 1993-1996 involving the factions mentioned in this report, as well as the Taliban. This information will be supplied to the Afghan Independent Human Rights Commission and the U.N. Office for the High Commissioner for Human Rights, in Geneva.

Violations of International Humanitarian Law

The Afshar campaign was marked by widespread and serious violations of international humanitarian law. War crimes included attacks on the civilian population and civilian objects, killings, torture and other inhumane treatment, rape, abductions and forced disappearances, forced labor, and pillage and looting. As discussed in Section IV below, there is compelling evidence that the senior Ittihad and Jamiat commanders involved in the Afshar campaign are implicated in these violations.[231] It is also possible that some commanders may be liable for crimes against humanity. Illegal acts that were part of a widespread or systematic attack on a civilian population, such as the killing or abduction of members of certain minorities, may amount to crimes against humanity.

Abdul Rabb al-Rasul Sayyaf, the overall leader of Ittihad, is implicated in the war crimes documented above either directly or indirectly, as a matter of command responsibility. As a senior leader of Ittihad, Sayyaf controlled all Ittihad commanders throughout the Afshar attack. Witnesses, including a soldier who fought with Ittihad, say that they saw Sayyaf coordinating military operations during the campaign and meeting with sub-commanders.[232] Sayyaf met with senior Ittihad commanders in Paghman the day before the Afshar campaign to discuss the Afshar attack.[233] Sayyaf was also present at the meeting convened by Massoud in the Hotel Intercontinental on the second day of the Afshar operation on February 12.[234] His leadership role in Ittahad as well as his involvement in planning the Afshar campaign place him in the position of being directly responsible for abuses or culpable under the doctrine of command responsibility.

Other Ittihad commanders are potentially implicated. Several officials, journalists, and military commanders described how Ittihad commanders Shir Alam, Zalmay Tofan,

---

[231] For more information on the specific legal standards of international humanitarian law applicable to the Afshar campaign, and the culpability of individual commanders, see section IV below.

[232] Human Rights Watch interview with K.M.B., former combatant who served under Ittihad forces, Kabul, July 4, 2003; See AJP report, January 2005, p. 30.

[233] See AJP report, January 2005, p. 29.

[234] See AJP report, January 2005, p. 30.

Mullah Taj Mohammad, Abdullah Wardak, "Doctor" Abdullah, and Abdullah Shah had effective control over troops engaged in abductions and street fighting with Wahdat forces in west Kabul, and said that they commanded troops at Afshar.[235] Commanders Khanjar and Patang were said to have been commanding troops at Afshar.[236] One witness who was abducted and put into forced labor in Paghman under Ittihad troops saw and spoke with Zalmay Tofan while in captivity, pleading for medical assistance.[237] Witnesses interviewed by Human Rights Watch and the Afghan Justice Project claim that they saw Zalmay Tofan, Shir Alam, "Doctor" Abdullah, and Abdullah Shah leading troops on the ground during the Afshar campaign.[238] One witness cited above, who was abducted by Ittihad forces, said he was under the control of an Ittihad commander named Shir Agha Zarshakh, who was leading a group of soldiers.[239] The Afghan Justice Project interviewed witnesses who identified other commanders who were seen directing troops during the Afshar campaign, including "Doctor" Abdullah and Khanjar, as well as other Ittihad commanders, including Jaglan Naeem, Abdul Manan Diwana, Amanullah Kochi, Shirin, Mushtaq Lalai, and Mullah Kachkol.[240] According to one witness interviewed by the Afghan Justice Project, two senior Ittihad commanders—Shir Alam and Zalmay Tofan—were at the meeting convened by Massoud the day before the Afshar attack.[241]

Several Jamiat commanders, including Massoud, Fahim, Baba Jalander, Bismullah Khan, Baba Jan, Ahmadi Takhari, Kabir Andarabi, and Mullah Ezat, were directly involved in the 1993 Afshar campaign, according to officials who worked within the Rabbani

---

[235] Human Rights Watch interview with H.A.W., former official in the interim government 1992-1993, Kabul, July 23, 2003; Human Rights Watch interview with S.A.R., July 11, 2003; Human Rights Watch interview with R.D., July 16, 2003; Human Rights Watch interview with C.S.A., July 18, 2003.

[236] Human Rights Watch interview with K.S., former government security official, Kabul, July 24, 2003 ("Khanjar and Patang were direct operational commanders."); Human Rights Watch interview with C.S.A., July 18, 2003.

[237] Human Rights Watch interview with A.Q.L., Afshar resident, July 21, 2003.

[238] Human Rights Watch interview with A.S.F., Tajik Afshar resident who traveled in and out of Afshar during February 11-16, 1993, Kabul, July 2, 2003; Human Rights Watch interview with Q.E.K., former Wahdat political official who witnessed the attack, Kabul, July 15, 2003. See AJP report, January 2005, p. 28.

[239] The following quotes are taken from a Human Rights Watch interview with L.S., July 4, 2003.

[240] AJP report, January 2005, p. 28.

[241] Ibid., p. 29.

government in 1992-1993.[242]   General Fahim, who was chief of the Afghan intelligence service in 1992-1993 but controlled several military posts as well, was one of the chief commanders under Massoud. Officials in the Rabbani government in 1992-1993 told Human Rights Watch that Fahim was directly involved in the Afshar attack, controlled at least one of the military posts on Television Mountain throughout the period of this report, and that he was involved in the planning of the Afshar campaign and took part in negotiations with Harakat commanders to gain their cooperation before the attack.[243] The same officials said Mullah Ezat and Anwar Dangar were also involved in the Afshar campaign.

---

[242] Human Rights Watch interview with S.A.R., former Shura-e Nazar official in 1992, Kabul, July 11, 2003; Human Rights Watch interview with R.D., former official in the interim government 1992-1995, Kabul, July 16, 2003; Human Rights Watch interview with C.S.A., former government security official, July 18, 2003.

[243] Human Rights Watch interview with S.A.R., July 11, 2003 ("Fahim had two headquarters: one at Karte Mamorin, near Bagh Bala, another near Karte Sakhi or Karte Parwan. The night before [the attack on Afshar], he went there to see what was going on. Massoud went to TV mountain. Fahim and Massoud commanded the bombardment from there."); Human Rights Watch interview with R.D., July 16, 2003 ("Fahim was directly involved [at Afshar]; he was directly above the other commanders. Fahim and Massoud were in Bagh Bala, which was the headquarters [during the attack]."); Human Rights Watch interview with C.S.A., July 18, 2003 ("Fahim controlled the deal [for Harakat to turn over Afshar mountain].").

IV. Culpability

The attacks on civilians, summary executions, torture, abductions and looting documented in this report were not spontaneous events or inevitable consequences of war. They were war crimes committed by troops within military structures with command-and-control mechanisms. And in many cases documented here, the actions or omissions of commanders resulted in or facilitated war crimes. There is compelling evidence that factional leaders either knew or should have known of ongoing serious abuses being committed by their troops, and in many cases failed to take steps to stop them.

This section describes the applicable law that governs the hostilities in 1992-1993 and outlines the command-and-control structure of each of the parties discussed in this report and the possible individual criminal responsibility of each party's main commanders.

A. Applicable law

This report describes hostilities that took place among various Afghan political-military factions after the withdrawal of Soviet forces from Afghanistan. As such, they are considered under international humanitarian law (the laws of war) to be a non-international armed conflict—i.e., not a conflict between two states—also known as an internal armed conflict or civil war.

The primary law applicable to non-international (internal) armed conflicts is article 3 common to the four Geneva Conventions of 1949.[244] Afghanistan ratified the Geneva Conventions in 1956. The Second Additional Protocol to the Geneva Conventions

---

[244] Geneva Convention for the Amelioration of the Condition of the Wounded and Sick in Armed Forces in the Field (First Geneva Convention), 75 U.N.T.S. 31, entered into force Oct. 21, 1950; Geneva Convention for the Amelioration of the Condition of Wounded, Sick and Shipwrecked Members of Armed Forces at Sea (Second Geneva Convention), 75 U.N.T.S. 85, entered into force Oct. 21, 1950; Geneva Convention relative to the Treatment of Prisoners of War (Third Geneva Convention), 75 U.N.T.S. 135, entered into force Oct. 21, 1950; Geneva Convention relative to the Protection of Civilian Persons in Time of War (Fourth Geneva Convention), 75 U.N.T.S. 287, entered into force Oct. 21, 1950.

(Protocol II),[245] applicable to non-international armed conflicts, has not been ratified by Afghanistan. Still, most if not all of its provisions are recognized as reflective of customary international law (and were so recognized in 1992-1993). In addition, certain provisions of Protocol I of the Geneva Conventions applicable to international armed conflict,[246] including many of those concerned with protection of civilian populations, are also considered reflective of customary international law applicable at the time to non-international armed conflicts.[247]

International humanitarian law in civil armed conflicts is legally binding on both government forces and armed opposition groups. Forces within the recognized Afghan government that was formed after the collapse of the Najibullah government included Jamiat, Ittihad, and (at certain times) Wahdat and Junbish. Non-state forces fighting against the government included Hezb-e Islami and, by 1993, Wahdat.

In addition to violations of international humanitarian law amounting to war crimes, "crimes against humanity" may also have been committed. Crimes against humanity refer to acts that, by their scale or nature, outrage the conscience of humankind. Crimes against humanity were first codified in the charter of the Nuremberg Tribunal of 1945. Since then, the concept has been incorporated into a number of international treaties, including the Rome Statute of the International Criminal Court (ICC). Although a single legal definition of crimes against humanity did not exist in 1992-1993, there was and has been broad agreement that crimes against humanity are unlawful acts, such as murder, torture, dissapparances and rape, committed as part of a widespread or systematic attack against a civilian population by a state or non-state actor.[248]

---

[245] Protocol Additional to the Geneva Conventions of 12 August 1949, and Relating to the Protection of Victims of Non-International Armed Conflicts (Protocol II), 1125 U.N.T.S. 609, *entered into force* Dec. 7, 1978.

[246] Protocol Additional to the Geneva Conventions of 12 August 1949, and Relating to the Protection of Victims of International Armed Conflicts (Protocol I), 1125 U.N.T.S. 3, entered into force Dec. 7, 1978.

[247] See International Law Commission, Draft Code of Crimes against the Peace and Security of Mankind (1996), art. 20, e-g. See also, Dieter Fleck (ed.), *The Handbook of Humanitarian Law in Armed Conflict* (Oxford: Oxford University Press, 1995), p. 120. For an authoritative analysis of customary international humanitarian law, based on an extensive study coordinated by the International Committee of the Red Cross, see Jean-Marie Henckaerts and Louise Doswald-Beck, *Customary International Humanitarian Law* (Cambridge: Cambridge University Press, 2005), hereinafter "ICRC, *Customary International Humanitarian Law*."

[248] For more on legal definitions of crimes against humanity, see M. Cherif Bassiouni, *Crimes Against Humanity in International Humanitarian Law* (The Hague: Kluwer Law International, 1999). See also, "Article 18: Crimes against Humanity" in chapter II, "Draft Code of Crimes Against the Peace and

International human rights standards are also applicable in times of conflict. During armed conflicts, international humanitarian law, as the *lex specialis* or specialized law, takes precedence but does not replace human rights law. Persons under the control of government or armed opposition forces in an internal armed conflict must in all cases be treated in accordance with international humanitarian law, which incorporates important human rights standards. And where that law is absent, vague, or inapplicable, human rights law still applies. Human rights law can be found, for instance, in the International Covenant on Civil and Political Rights[249] and the Convention against Torture and other Cruel, Inhuman or Degrading Treatment or Punishment,[250] both of which had been ratified by Afghanistan.

Specific protections

A fundamental rule of international humanitarian law is that civilians enjoy general protection against danger arising from military operations. The rule of "civilian immunity" is binding on all parties to a conflict, regardless of whether the conflict is international or non-international in character.[251]

The principle of civilian immunity has been codified in numerous treaties. One of the clearest expressions of the principle is set out in article 51(2) of Additional Protocol I to the Geneva Conventions, which states:

> The civilian population as such, as well as individual civilians, shall not be the object of attack. Acts or threats of violence, the primary purpose of which is to spread terror among the civilian population, are prohibited.[252]

Security of Mankind" in the *International Law Commission Report*, 1996 at www.un.org/law/ilc/reports/1996/chap02.htm#doc3 (accessed July 2004).

[249] International Covenant on Civil and Political Rights (ICCPR), opened for signature December 16, 1966, 999 U.N.T.S. 171 (entered into force March 23, 1976, and acceded to by Afghanistan on January 24, 1983).

[250] Convention against Torture and Other Cruel, Inhuman or Degrading Treatment or Punishment, G.A. Res. 39/46, annex, 39, U.N. Doc. A/39/51 (entered into force June 26, 1987; ratified by Afghanistan on April 1, 1987).

[251] See ICRC, *Customary International Humanitarian Law*, rules 1-8. Fleck (ed.), *The Handbook of Humanitarian Law in Armed Conflict*, p. 120: "The general prohibition against indiscriminate warfare applies independently of Arts. 48 and 51 [of Protocol I]. The relevant provisions of the Additional Protocols merely codify pre-existing customary law, because the principle of distinction belongs to the oldest fundamental maxims of established customary rules of humanitarian law."

[252] Protocol I, art. 51(2). Similar language is found in Protocol II, art. 13(2).

Civilians are protected at all times from attack unless they take a direct part in the hostilities.[253] Although a precise definition of taking "direct part in hostilities" does not exist, it has generally come to mean acts that are intended to cause actual harm to the enemy, such as using or loading weapons. Providing food or other assistance to armed groups, or expressing sympathy for one side, does not deprive civilians of their civilian immunity.[254]

Civilian objects, such as residences, schools and mosques, are also protected from attack, except for such time that they are military objectives. A civilian object becomes a military target during the period it is used for military purposes.[255]

Parties to a conflict must make affirmative efforts to distinguish between civilian objects and military targets, as stated in article 48 of Protocol I:

> In order to ensure respect for and protection of the civilian population and civilian objects, the Parties to the conflict shall at all times distinguish between the civilian population and combatants, and between civilian objects and military objectives, and accordingly shall direct their operations only against military objectives.[256]

Parties to a conflict are specifically obligated to direct attacks only at military targets. Attacks that are "indiscriminate" are prohibited. Indiscriminate attacks are "those which are not directed against a military objective," "those which employ a method or means of combat which cannot be directed at a specific military objective," or "those which employ a method or means of combat, the effects of which cannot be limited," and consequently, are "of a nature to strike military objectives and civilians or civilian objects without distinction."[257]

Article 51(5) of Protocol I details some of the characteristics of indiscriminate attacks:

---

[253] See Protocol I, art. 51(3); Protocol II, art. 13(3).

[254] See ICRC, *Customary International Humanitarian Law*, rules 6.

[255] See Protocol I, article 52(1), which reflects customary law for international armed conflicts. See ICRC, *Customary International Humanitarian Law*, rules 9-10.

[256] Protocol I, art. 48. "Military objectives" are defined as "those objects, which by their nature, location, purpose or use make an effective contribution to military action." Protocol I, art. 52(2).

[257] Protocol I, art. 51. See ICRC, *Customary International Humanitarian Law*, rules 11-13.

Among others, the following types of attacks are to be considered as indiscriminate:

> (a) an attack by bombardment by any methods or means which treats as a single military objective a number of clearly separated and distinct military objectives located in a city, town, village or other area containing a similar concentration of civilians or civilian objects; and

> (b) an attack which may be expected to cause incidental loss of civilian life, injury to civilians, damage to civilian objects, or a combination thereof, which would be excessive in relation to the concrete and direct military advantage anticipated.[258]

In addition, common article 3 to the four Geneva Conventions, applicable in non-international armed conflicts, specifically outlaws killings and mistreatment of civilians and captured combatants. Prohibited in particular are "violence to life and person . . . murder of all kinds, mutilation, cruel treatment and torture; taking of hostages; [and] outrages upon personal dignity, in particular humiliating and degrading treatment."[259]

In addition to the protections found in common article 3, customary international humanitarian law applicable in internal armed conflicts provides civilians and captured combatants a number of fundamental guarantees. Those particularly relevant to the situation in Afghanistan in 1992-1993 include prohibitions against enforced disappearance, rape and other forms of sexual violence, arbitrary deprivation of liberty, and forced labor.[260]

Enforced disappearance, though not defined under international humanitarian law, encompasses the prohibitions against arbitrary detention, inhumane treatment, and murder.[261] It also encompasses the right of those deprived of their liberty during a

---

[258] Protocol I, art. 51(5).

[259] See e.g., Geneva Convention relative to the Protection of Civilian Persons in Time of War (Fourth Geneva Convention), art. 3. See also Protocol II, art. 4.

[260] See generally ICRC, *Customary International Humanitarian Law*, chapter 32.

[261] See ICRC, *Customary International Humanitarian Law*, rule 98; see also Declaration on the Protection of All Persons from Enforced Disappearances, G.A. res. 47/133, 47 U.N. GAOR Supp. (No. 49) at 207, U.N. Doc. A/47/49 (1992).

conflict by a government or an armed group to have their personal details be registered. From this emerges a duty to investigate cases of alleged enforced disappearance.[262]

Rape and other forms of sexual violence have long been prohibited under international humanitarian law.[263] While not explicitly mentioned in common article 3 to the Geneva Conventions, rape is considered part of the article's prohibition against "violence to life and person," including cruel treatment and torture and "outrages upon personal dignity."[264] The Fourth Geneva Convention on the protection of civilians and Protocol II explicitly prohibit rape.[265] The statutes for the ad hoc and permanent international criminal courts have reaffirmed the prohibition against rape and other sexual violence as a war crime and as a crime against humanity.[266]

The arbitrary deprivation of liberty is prohibited during internal armed conflicts. Arbitrary detention is considered imcompatible with the requirement of humane treatment under common article 3 to the Geneva Conventions.[267]

Forced labor that is uncompensated or abusive is prohibited.[268]

Pillage and looting can also amount to war crimes. During an internal armed conflict, destroying or seizing the private property of civilians is prohibited unless there is a

---

[262] ICRC, *Customary International Humanitarian Law*, rule 123.

[263] See *Instructions for the Government of Armies of the United States in the Field*, prepared by Francis Lieber, promulgated as General Order no. 100 by U.S. President Abraham Lincoln, April 24, 1863 (Lieber Code), art. 44.

[264] See common article 3 to the Geneva Conventions. Additional Protocol I, article 75, likewise prohibits "outrages upon personal dignity" and "humiliating and degrading treatment, enforced prostitution and any form of indecent assault."

[265] Fourth Geneva Convention, art. 27; Protocol II, art. 4.

[266] Article 5 of the Statute of the International Criminal Tribunal for the former Yugoslavia (ICTY) and article 3 of the Statute of the International Criminal Tribunal for Rwanda (ICTR) both include widespread and systematic rape as a set of acts which can amount to a crime against humanity. See ICTY Statute, adopted May 5, 1993, at http://www.un.org/icty/legaldoc/index.htm and ICTR statute, at http://ictr.org/ENGLISH/basicdocs/statute/2004.pdf. Article 7 of the Statute for the International Criminal Court states that widespread and systematic rape, sexual slavery, enforced prostitution, and other forms of sexual violence can amount to a crime against humanity. See Rome Statute of the International Criminal Court, 37 I.L.M. 999 (1998), article 7.

[267] ICRC, *Customary International Humanitarian Law*, rule 99.

[268] See ICRC, *Customary International Humanitarian Law*, rule 95.

militarily necessary reason for doing so. Pillage, the forcible taking or destruction of property for private purposes, is strictly forbidden. Looting can be defined as the taking of property without the direct use of force. Both pillage and looting violate the general prohibition against theft.[269]

Civilians are also protected by basic human rights law. In cases where civilians are in the control of parties acting in the capacity of a sovereign power, those parties are obligated to uphold human rights norms, including the right to life; the prohibition against torture and cruel, inhumane, and degrading treatment; prohibitions against slavery and forced labor; rights to liberty and security of person; and rights of detainees to due process, among others.[270] Parties must respect these human rights norms without making distinctions based on ethnic or religious status.[271]

Individual Criminal Responsibility

All individuals, including factional leaders, military commanders, soldiers and civilians, are subject to prosecution for war crimes, crimes against humanity, and applicable domestic crimes.

Individual criminal responsibility for war crimes committed during internal armed conflicts has been explicitly provided in a number of international treaties since the early 1990s. These include the statutes for the international criminal tribunals for the former Yugoslavia and Rwanda, as well as the international criminal court, and multilateral treaties such as Amended Protocol II to the Convention on Certain Conventional Weapons.

During the armed conflict in Afghanistan, various entities called on all parties to the conflict to respect international humanitarian law. The ICRC, in a press release on May 5, 1992, appealed "to all parties to respect international humanitarian law and to ensure respect for its rules by everyone involved in the fighting." This appeal was repeated in August of that year.[272] (Later, in March 1994, the U.N. Security Council issued a statement on the

---

[269] See generally, ICRC, *Customary International Humanitarian Law*, chapter 16; Theodor Meron, Human Rights and Humanitarian Norms as Customary Law (Oxford: Clarendon Press, 1989), pp. 46-47.

[270] ICCPR, art. 6 (right to life), art. 7 (prohibition against torture and cruel, inhumane and degrading treatment) art. 8 (prohibition against slavery and forced labor), art. 9 (right to liberty and security of person), art. 10 (rights of due process). See also Convention against Torture and Other Cruel, Inhuman or Degrading Treatment or Punishment, arts. 1 and 2.

[271] See ICCPR, art. 2(1).

[272] ICRC, Press Release no. 1712, May 5, 1992, cited in ICRC, *Customary International Humanitarian Law*, vol. 2, ch. 43, sec. 138.

situation in Afghanistan in which it "stresse[d] the importance that it attaches to full compliance with international humanitarian law in all its aspects and recalls that those who violate international humanitarian law bear individual responsibility."[273])

Persons who commit war crimes may be held criminally liable. They may also be held criminally responsible for assisting in, facilitating, aiding, or abetting the commission of a war crime. They can also be prosecuted for planning or instigating the commission of a war crime.[274] In addition, leaders, commanders and troops who deliberately order or commit widespread or systematic murder, enslavement, mutilation, or rape of civilians can also be held individually liable for crimes against humanity. Crimes against humanity give rise to universal jurisdiction, do not have a statue of limitations, and do not admit the defense of following superior orders.

Commanders and other leaders may be criminally responsible for war crimes or crimes against humanity committed by troops under their command. The responsibility of superior officers for crimes commited by their subordinates is known as command responsibility. Although the concept originated in military law, it now also includes the responsibility of civil authorities for abuses committed by persons under their authority. The doctrine of command responsibility was part of customary international law in 1992-1993 and has been upheld in decisions by the international criminal tribunals for the former Yugoslavia and for Rwanda, and is today codified in the Rome Statute for the International Criminal Court.[275]

There are two forms of command responsibility. The first is direct responsibility for orders that are unlawful, such as when a military commander authorizes or orders rapes, massacres, or intentional attacks on civilians. In this case, the commander's forces are an instrument of the commander's will, and he is directly culpable as he would be if he carried out the abuses with his own hands. Having ordered such a crime, a commander can be found liable so long as the crime was attempted, even if it was not actually committed.[276]

---

[273] U.N. Security Council Statement, March 23, 1994) S/PRST/1994/12.

[274] ICRC, *Customary International Humanitarian Law,* rule 151.

[275] See footnote 278 below, on the Celebici case.

[276] ICRC, *Customary International Humanitarian Law,* rule 152.

All combatants have a duty to disobey manifestly unlawful orders. Obeying superior orders does not relieve a subordinate of criminal responsibility so long as he knew or should have known that the orders were unlawful.[277]

The second form of command responsibility is imputed responsibility, when a superior failed to prevent or punish crimes committed by a subordinate acting on his own initiative. This second kind of responsibility depends on whether the superior knew or had reason to know of the subordinates' crimes, and was in a position to stop and punish them. A commander has "reason to know" when offenses were so numerous or notorious that a reasonable person would conclude that the commander must have known of their commission. If a commander had such notice, he can be held criminally responsible for his subordinates if he failed to take appropriate measures to control the subordinates, to prevent their atrocities, and to punish offenders.

For the doctrine of command responsibility to be applicable, two conditions must be met. A *de facto* superior-subordinate relationship must exist, and the superior must exercise effective control over the subordinate. Effective control includes the ability to give orders or instructions, to ensure their implementation, and to punish or discipline subordinates if the orders are disobeyed.[278]

B. Culpability of specific individuals

The militias and political-military parties implicated in the abuses outlined in this report include the Jamiat, Ittihad, Hezb-e Islami, Wahdat, Harakat, and Junbish factions.[279] This section discusses the specific culpability of these factions' commanders in the abuses documented in this report. This section also discusses (in the Jamiat and Shura-e

---

[277] ICRC, *Customary International Humanitarian Law,* rules 154-55.

[278] The International Criminal Tribunal for the former Yugoslavia (ICTY) has defined "effective control" under existing international law as the superior "having the material ability to prevent and punish the commission" of violations of international humanitarian law:

The doctrine of command responsibility is ultimately predicated upon the power of the superior to control the acts of his subordinates. A duty is placed upon the superior to exercise this power so as to prevent and repress the crimes committed by subordinates. . . . It follows that there is a threshold at which persons cease to possess the necessary powers of control over the actual perpetrators of offense and, accordingly, cannot properly be considered their "superiors."

Prosecutor v. Delali, Judgment no. IT-96-21-T, Nov. 16,1998 (Celebici case), para. 377-378. See also *Prosecutor v. Karanac, Kunac and Vokovic.* Judgment no. IT-96-23-T & IT-96-23/1-T, Nov. 22, 2001, para. 396.

[279] See Appendix A for more information on these groups.

Nazar entry below) the governmental structure under Sibghatullah Mujaddidi and Burhanuddin Rabbani, the successive presidents of Afghanistan in 1992-1993.

What follows below is not meant to provide a comprehensive legal analysis of the ultimate criminal responsibility of the individuals named. Considerably more investigative work needs to be done to establish the criminal culpability of the various commanders and leaders implicated in the war crimes documented in this report. By laying the basic groundwork, however, we hope to encourage full criminal investigations and show that such investigations are both necessary and possible.

Wahdat

During the period discussed in this report, Wahdat forces were under the overall command of Abdul Ali Mazari (killed in 1995).[280] Abdul Karim Khalili (as of mid-2005 one of the two vice-presidents under President Hamid Karzai) served as Mazari's deputy (he later took over Wahdat after Mazari's death). Second-tier Wahdat commanders in Kabul included Abdul Wahid Turkmani, Mohsin Sultani, Tahir Tofan, Sedaqat Jahori, and Commander Bahrami. Wahdat's two main commanders in west Kabul were Shafi Dawana ("Shafi the Mad") and Nasir Dawana ("Nasir the Mad").

As was shown in section III (A) above, Wahdat forces repeatedly launched military attacks in West Kabul in 1992-1993, primarily against Ittihad forces. During these battles, there is compelling evidence that Wahdat forces failed to make efforts to distinguish between civilian objects and military targets, and that forces often fired small and heavy weapons indiscriminately into the dense civilian setting of west Kabul. In several cases documented here, Wahdat forces appear to have intentionally targeted civilians or civilian areas with gunfire, rockets. and mortar fire.

In addition, section III (A) and parts of section III (C) of this report show that Wahdat factions engaged in a pattern and practice of abductions and arbitary detentions, usually directed at civilians and apparently based on ethnic animus. Many of those detained by

---

[280] Information on the command structure of Wahdat is based on numerous interviews with Wahdat officials and other sources familiar with events in 1992-1993. Human Rights Watch interview with S.K., Afghan medical worker in Karte Seh (West Kabul) during early 1990's, Kabul, July 9, 2003; Human Rights Watch interview with S.A.R., former Shura-e Nazar official in 1992, Kabul, July 11, 2003; Human Rights Watch interview with Q.E.K., former Wahdat official, Kabul, July 15, 2003; Human Rights Watch interview with R.D., former official in the interim government 1992-1995, Kabul, July 16, 2003; Human Rights Watch interview with C.S.A., former government security official, July 18, 2003. The command structure of Wahdat is also discussed by the Afghan Justice Project, see AJP report, January 2005, pp. 34-36.

Wahdat—mostly Pashtuns—were severely mistreated or forced to work, and in several cases shown here, Wahdat executed civilian prisoners.

As noted above, willful killing of civilians is a war crime. Commanders involved in specific commissions of these crimes, and factional leaders who ordered abuses, are responsible under international criminal law and can be prosecuted. Higher-level Wahdat commanders not directly involved in abuses, who nonetheless had effective control over troops implicated in abuses and knew or should have known about the abuses and failed to take action to stop them, may also be liable as a matter of command responsibility.

Commanders in Wahdat may also be liable for crimes against humanity as the killings and abductions documented in this report appear to have been part of widespread and systematic attacks directed at a distinct civilian population. Wahdat commanders may be liable specifically because of their ethnic persecution—the fact that their forces appear to have targeted non-Hazara civilians for killing and abduction based on their ethnicity. There is compelling evidence that prisoners taken by Wahdat—mostly Pashtuns—were chosen from other civilians on the basis of their ethnic identity. As shown in section III (A) above, troops engaging in abuses often appear to have surmised the ethnicity of victims on the basis of their appearance, language, or accent, and decided to abuse them based on their ethnicity. Statements and actions of Wahdat officials confirmed that civilians were being arrested due to their ethnicity, suggesting a policy or a plan. As cited in Section III (A) above, Mazari and Karim Khalili each acknowledged taking Pashtun civilians as prisoners, in interviews with Reuters and Associated Press.[281]

Wahdat forces, along with the other factions discussed in this report, are also implicated in numerous acts of murder, pillage, and looting in violation of international humanitarian law. The failures by commanders to stop or prevent the abuses could make them complicit in the violations as a matter of command responsibility.

Further investigation is needed into the command-and-control structures of Wahdat forces and the specific culpability of each of its main commanders who are still alive. Mazari, Shafi Dawana and Nasir Dawana are all deceased, but Wahid Turkmani, Mohsin Sultani, Tahir Tofan, Sedaqat Jahori, and Commander Bahrami are believed to be still alive, and should be investigated for their role in the Wahdat abuses documented here.

---

[281] Andrew Roche, "Kabul fighting erupts again despite ceasefire," Reuters, June 4, 1992; Sharon Herbaugh, "Civilians tell of captivity, torture by rebels," Associated Press, June 6, 1992.

Ittihad

Ittihad forces in 1992-1993 were under the overall command of Abdul Rabb al-Rasul Sayyaf. Second-tier Ittihad commanders included Shir Alam (parliamentary candidate and as of mid-2005 a senior commander in the defense ministry), Zalmay Tofan (until mid-2005 a senior commander in the defense ministry), Mullah Taj Mohammad (as of mid-2005, parliamentary candidate, head of political group called the Kabul Citizen's Counsel; governor of Kabul in 2003-2004), Abdullah Wardak (former minister of martyrs and disabled in President Karzai's interim 2002-2004 cabinet), "Doctor" Abdullah (as of mid-2005 a commander in the ministry of defense; no relation to Dr. Abdullah, the current foreign minister of Afghanistan), and Abdullah Shah (executed by the Afghan government in April 2004).[282] Other commanders reported to hold senior positions were Khanjar (deceased), Patang, Jaglan Naeem (as of mid-2005 reported to be serving as an official in the ministry of interior), Abdul Manan Diwana (as of mid-2005 reported to be governor of a district in Sar-e Pol province), Noor Aqi (reported to be serving as an official in the ministry of defense), Amanullah Kochi, Shirin, Mushtaq Lalai, and Mullah Kachkol (as of mid-2005 reported to be parliamentary candidate and commander in the ministry of defense).[283]

As shown in Section III (A) above, Ittihad forces repeatedly launched military attacks against Wahdat in 1992-1993. During these attacks they failed to make efforts to distinguish between civilian objects and military targets. Ittihad forces regularly fired small and heavy weapons indiscriminately within the dense civilian setting of west Kabul. In several cases, Ittihad forces appear to have intentionally targeted civilians or civilian areas with gunfire or rockets and mortar fire.

In addition, as shown in section III (A), Ittihad factions engaged in a regular pattern and practice of abduction based on ethnic grounds, usually directed at Hazara civilians. Many of those detained by Ittihad were severely mistreated or forced to work. There is clear and compelling evidence in section III (C) that during the February 1993 Afshar campaign, Ittihad forces specifically engaged in widespread killing and abduction of

---

[282] Information on the command structure of Ittihad is based on numerous interviews with sources familiar with events in 1992-1993. Human Rights Watch interview with S.A.R., former Shura-e Nazar official in 1992, Kabul, July 11, 2003; Human Rights Watch interview with Q.E.K., former Wahdat official, Kabul, July 15, 2003; Human Rights Watch interview with R.D., former official in the interim government 1992-1995, Kabul, July 16, 2003; Human Rights Watch interview with C.S.A., former government security official, July 18, 2003. The command structure of Ittihad is also discussed by the Afghan Justice Project, see AJP report, January 2005, pp. 28-29.

[283] Human Rights Watch telephone interviews with numerous Afghan journalists and observers in Kabul, May 2005; AJP report, January 2005, pp. 28-29.

Hazara civilians. As shown in section III (C), Ittihad forces during the Afshar operation specifically targeted Hazara civilians for killing or abduction, based on their ethnicity.

The acts detailed above amount to war crimes. Commanders involved in specific commissions of these crimes, and factional leaders who ordered abuses, are liable and can be prosecuted. Higher-level Ittihad commanders not directly involved in abuses, who nonetheless had effective control over troops implicated in abuses and knew or should have known about the abuses and failed to take action to stop them, may also be liable on command responsibility grounds.

Commanders in Ittihad may also be liable for crimes against humanity, as the killings and abductions documented in this report appear to have been part of widespread or systematic attacks directed at a distinct civilian population. Ittihad commanders may be liable specifically because of their ethnic persecution—the fact that their forces appear to have targeted Hazara civilians for killing and abduction based on their ethnicity. There is compelling evidence, especially with respect to the Afshar operation, that most prisoners taken by Ittihad—Hazaras—were chosen from other civilians on the basis of their ethnic identity, as troops engaging in abuses appear to have surmised the ethnicity of victims on the basis of their appearance, language, or accent, as repeatedly demonstrated in sections III (A) and III (C) above. Investigations are needed to determine whether these ethnically motivated abuses were part of an Ittihad plan or policy or were merely the spontaneous acts of their troops on the ground.

As noted throughout section III, Ittihad forces, along with the other factions discussed in this report, are also implicated in numerous acts of murder, pillage, and looting in violation of international humanitarian law. The failures by commanders to stop or prevent the abuses could make them legally responsible as a matter of command responsibility.

All of the Ittihad commanders named above are alive as of mid-2005, except for Patang, who was reportedly killed in 2004, and commander Abdullah Shah, who, as noted above, was executed by the Afghan government in April 2004.[284]

---

[284] Abdullah Shah was convicted after a hasty murder trial criticized by the Afghan Independent Human Rights Commission. Regardless of his past crimes, his testimony on other crimes and events would have been useful in other future trials. For more on the Abdullah Shah case, see AJP report, January 2005, footnote 30.

Abdul Rabb al-Rasul Sayyaf, the overall leader of Ittihad, is directly implicated in the abductions and the indiscriminate and intentional targeting of civilians documented in this report. As a senior leader of Ittihad, Sayyaf had effective control over all Ittihad commanders throughout the period covered here. Sayyaf thus exercised ultimate control of Ittihad forces who committed these abuses. As noted in section III (A) above, officials in the Rabbani government in 1992-1993, which was allied with Sayyaf, acknowledged to Human Rights Watch that Sayyaf was the senior military commander of Ittihad forces, that he was in regular contact with his commanders, and that he had the power to release prisoners held by his subordinates, and in fact ordered such releases on several occasions, demonstrating his command over those commanders.[285] Health workers in west Kabul told Human Rights Watch in 2003 of additional cases in which negotiators with the International Committee of the Red Cross spoke with Sayyaf to obtain the release of prisoners, further demonstrating his control over subordinate commanders.[286] Human Rights Watch also spoke with an individual who negotiated with Sayyaf to obtain a relative's release.[287] As noted in section III (A), in June 1992, when interviewed by a journalist in Kabul about abductions, Sayyaf did not deny that Ittihad forces were abducting Hazara civilians, but instead accused Wahdat of being an agent of the Iranian government.[288]

With respect to the Afshar atrocities, section III (C) also noted that persons, including a soldier who fought with Ittihad, told Human Rights Watch that they saw Sayyaf coordinating military operations during the Afshar campaign and meeting with his sub-commanders.[289] As noted in section III (C) above, Sayyaf reportedly met with senior Ittihad commanders in Paghman the day before the Afshar campaign to discuss the Afshar attack.[290] Sayyaf was also present at a meeting convened by Massoud in the Hotel

---

[285] Human Rights Watch interview with S.A.R., former Shura-e Nazar official in 1992, Kabul, July 11, 2003; Human Rights Watch interview with R.D., former official in the interim government 1992-1995, Kabul, July 16, 2003; Human Rights Watch interview with C.S.A., former government security official, July 18, 2003.

[286] Human Rights Watch interview with H.K., aid worker, Kabul, July 5, 2003; Human Rights Watch interview with S.K., Afghan medical worker in Karte Seh (West Kabul) during early 1990's, Kabul, July 9, 2003.

[287] Human Rights Watch interview with L.R.G., Kabul, July 3, 2003.

[288] See Roche, "Kabul fighting erupts again despite ceasefire," Reuters, June 4, 1992

[289] Human Rights Watch interview with K.M.B., former combatant who served under Ittihad forces, Kabul, July 4, 2003; See AJP report, January 2005, p. 30.

[290] See AJP report, January 2005, p. 29.

Intercontinental on the second day of the Afshar operation on February 12.[291] These facts amount to compelling evidence that Sayyaf knew or should have known about Ittihad abuses during the campaign.

Other Ittihad commanders may be implicated in Ittihad abuses. As noted in Sections III (A) and (C) above, several officials, journalists, and military commanders described to Human Rights Watch how Ittihad commanders Shir Alam, Zalmay Tofan, Mullah Taj Mohammad, Abdullah Wardak, "Doctor" Abdullah, and Abdullah Shah had effective control over troops responsible for abductions and mistreatment of detainees during street fighting with Wahdat forces in west Kabul, and that they commanded troops at Afshar.[292] Commanders Khanjar and Patang were said to have been commanding troops at Afshar.[293] One witness who was abducted and put into forced labor in Paghman under Ittihad troops saw and spoke with Zalmay Tofan while in captivity, pleading for medical assistance.[294] Persons interviewed by Human Rights Watch and the Afghan Justice Project claim that they saw Zalmay Tofan, Shir Alam, Dr. Abdullah (Ittihad), and Abdullah Shah leading troops on the ground during the Afshar campaign.[295] The Afghan Justice Project interviewed persons who identified other commanders who were seen directing troops during the Afshar campaign, including Dr. Abdullah and Khanjar, as well as other Ittihad commanders, including Jaglan Naeem, Abdul Manan Diwana, Amanullah Kochi, Shirin, Mushtaq Lalai, and Mullah Kachkol.[296] According to one witness interviewed by the Afghan Justice Project, two senior Ittihad commanders—Shir Alam and Zalmay Tofan—were at the meeting convened by Massoud the day before the Afshar attack.[297]

---

[291] See AJP report, January 2005, p. 30.

[292] Human Rights Watch interview with H.A.W., former official in the interim government 1992-1993, Kabul, July 23, 2003; Human Rights Watch interview with S.A.R., July 11, 2003; Human Rights Watch interview with R.D., July 16, 2003; Human Rights Watch interview with C.S.A., July 18, 2003.

[293] Human Rights Watch interview with K.S., former government security official, Kabul, July 24, 2003 ("Khanjar and Patang were direct operational commanders."); Human Rights Watch interview with C.S.A., July 18, 2003.

[294] Human Rights Watch interview with A.Q.L., Afshar resident, July 21, 2003.

[295] Human Rights Watch interview with A.S.F., Tajik Afshar resident who traveled in and out of Afshar during February 11-16, 1993, Kabul, July 2, 2003; Human Rights Watch interview with Q.E.K., former Wahdat political official who witnessed the attack, Kabul, July 15, 2003. See AJP report, January 2005, p. 28.

[296] AJP report, January 2005, p. 28.

[297] Ibid., p. 29.

The exact role these Ittihad commanders played in the events described in this report requires further investigation. However, there is evidence that the command structure of Ittihad beneath Sayyaf is implicated in the abuses documented here. Both Sayyaf and his Ittihad commanders need to be thoroughly investigated regarding their role in the events described in this report.

Hezb-e Islami

Hezb-e Islami in 1992-1993 was headed by Gulbuddin Hekmatyar, whose current location is unknown. Forces consisted of the Kabul-based Firqa Sama; the Lashkar-e Isar (Army of Sacrifice), a conventional military force of over 6,000 troops Hekmatyer had organized in the late 1980s with the help of Pakistan and the United States; and other militias that joined these forces as the Najibullah regime collapsed in 1992.[298]

According to the Afghan Justice Project, which has researched the command structure of Hezb-e Islami, there was a Hezb-e Islami Shura Nizami (military council) under Hekmatyar, which consisted of ten to twelve members.[299] The Kabul-based commanders on the council were the Generals Faiz Mohammad (deceased) and Kashmir Khan (location unknown).[300] The Hezb-e Islami chief of staff was initially held by Commander Sabawon (as of mid-2005 an advisor to President Karzai), but shifted to Kashmir Khan sometime in 1992.[301] The chief artillery officer who supervised shelling and rocketing operation during late 1992 into 1993 was Toran Khalil.[302]

As shown in this report, Hezb-e Islami forces committed grave violations of international humanitarian law by intentionally targeting civilians and civilian areas for attack, or indiscriminately attacking areas in Kabul without distinguishing between civilian areas and military targets. Accounts and information presented in sections III (A) and III (B) show regular and repeated artillery strikes on civilian areas. Accounts and information in those sections also show that Hezb-e Islami regularly and repeatedly fired rockets into Kabul. As shown in those sections, Hezb-e Islami forces repeatedly used artillery and rockets in a manner suggesting that they were either intentionally targeting

---

[298] For more information about the composition of Hekmatyar's force in 1990-1992 and the role of Pakistan in its creation, see Coll, *Ghost Wars*, pp. 218 and 235-239; Rubin, *Fragmentation of Afghanistan*, pp. 252-253; AJP report, January 2005, p. 24.

[299] See AJP report, January 2005, p. 24.

[300] Ibid.

[301] Ibid.

[302] Ibid.

civilian sites, failing to aim at military objectives (with respect to artillery guns), or treating the whole city as one unified military target—any and all of which can amount to war crimes.

Hezb-e Islami's methods of attack and use of weapons systems demonstrate the abuses described above. With respect to artillery attacks, there was specific evidence in section III (A) above that Hezb-e Islami had the capacity to aim artillery at military targets, but purposefully or recklessly fired artillery at civilian objects instead, in violation of international humanitarian law. In numerous cases documented in this report, Hezb-e Islami forces fired artillery at civilian areas without clear military objectives, suggesting that they were either purposely targeting such areas, or recklessly aiming at Kabul as a whole.

As noted in Section III (A) above, Hekmatyar's forces also often used BM-40, BM-22, BM-12 rocket launchers and Sakr Soviet-made rockets in their attacks on Kabul. Such rocket systems are not designed for accuracy in close combat: they cannot be adequately aimed within urban settings or made to distinguish between military targets and civilian objects. The very use of such rocket systems within Kabul may have been in violation of international humanitarian law prohibitions on the use of inherently indiscriminate weapons.

As noted above, there is testimony in sections III (A) and III (B) that suggests that Hezb-e Islami and Hekmatyar were deliberately targeting the city of Kabul as a whole entity, to terrorize and kill civilians.

In addition, Hezb-e Islami, along with the other factions discussed in this report, are implicated in murders, pillage, and looting in violation of international humanitarian law. Hekmatyar and his commanders' failure to stop or prevent the abuses could make them responsible as a matter of command responsibility.

The head of Hezb-e Islami, Gulbuddin Hekmatyar, is centrally implicated in all of the crimes noted above. Hekmatyar was unambiguously the sole military and political leader of Hezb-e Islami, the Firqa Sama, and the Lashkar-e Isar (Army of Sacrifice), and was in command of Hezb-e Islami forces during its attacks on Kabul. Hekmatyar was the leader of Hezb-e Islami through the 1980s, and met regularly with Pakistani and U.S. intelligence officials, and even with American politicians who visited Pakistan in the

1980s.[303] Several mediators negotiated with Hekmatyar on peace initiatives in 1992 and 1993, as the head of Hezb-e Islami, and journalists repeatedly met with Hekmatyer in his capacity as the leader of Hezb-e Islami forces in the same period.[304] The then head of Pakistani Intelligence, Hamid Gul, negotiated with Hekmatyar in February 1993,[305] and again in March 1993.[306] Prince Turki al-Faisal, chief of Saudi Intelligence, and Asad Durrani, Director-General of Pakistan's Inter-Services Intelligence, negotiated between Hekmatyar and Ahmed Shah Massoud via radio in April 1992.[307]

Further investigation is needed into the sub-commanders of Hezb-e Islami who participated in the attacks on Kabul, to determine culpability for war crimes. As noted in section III (A) above, according to the Afghan Justice Project[308] the following commanders had operational control over the military posts reported to be firing artillery and rockets at Kabul during the period discussed in this report:

- o Commander Toran Khalil, chief artillery officer in Hezb-e Islami who supervised shelling and rocketing operations during late 1992 into 1993, commander of a base at an oil depot at the south of Charasiab, south of Kabul.

- o Toran Amanullah, commander of the Firqa Sama, stationed at the Rishkor military base, south of Kabul (as of mid-2005 in custody of the U.S. military).

---

[303] Hekmatyar met with Representative Charlie Wilson of Texas in 1984 and traveled to the United States the same year. See generally, George Crile, *Charlie Wilson's War: The Extraordinary Story of the Largest Covert Operation in History* (New York: Atlantic Monthly Press, 2003).

[304] Several journalists told Human Rights Watch about meeting with Hekmatyar in 1992 and 1993. Human Rights Watch interview with O.U., Afghan journalist, Kabul, July 13, 2003; Human Rights Watch interview with Suzy Price, correspondent for the British Broadcasting Corporation and Reuters, New York, April 3, 2004; Human Rights Watch telephone interviews with John Jennings, correspondent for Associated Press in 1992-1993, April 8 and 10, 2004; Human Right Watch telephone interview with Mark Urban, correspondent with the British Broadcasting Corporation in Kabul in 1992, April 29, 2004; Human Rights Watch telephone interview with Anthony Davis, correspondent for Jane's Defense Weekly in Kabul in 1992-1993, July 9, 2004.

[305] See John Jennings, "Afghanistan's Warring Rebel Factions Promise Temporary Truce," Associated Press, February 14, 1993.

[306] Kakar, *Afghanistan: The Soviet Invasion and Afghan Response* (Epilogue), p. 284.

[307] See Coll, *Ghost Wars*, p. 236 and accompanying footnotes 19-20 and cites. Osama Bin Laden, who was heavily involved in funding Arab mujahedin in the 1980s and knew Hekmatyar, also attempted to mediate by radio between Massoud and Hekmatyar.

[308] See AJP report, January 2005, pp. 23-24.

- Commander Zardad, commander of a military post at the Lycee Shorwaki (in mid-2005 on trial in the United Kingdom under universal jurisdication laws, for torture committed in Afghanistan in the 1990s).

- Engineer Zulmai, of the Lashkar Issar, commander of a post at the Kotal Hindki pass to the south of Chilsatoon, south of Kabul, near the Rishkor base (as of mid-2005 a government official in Nangahar province).

- Nur Rahman Panshiri, commander of a post in the village of Shahak, to the southeast of Kabul, directly controlled by the Sama division.

- General Wali Shah, an officer in the Najibullah government who joined Hezb-e Islami in 1992, commander of a base at Sang-e Nevishta, Logar, south of Kabul.

All of these commanders should be investigated for their role in the abuses described above. Further investigation is also needed into the roles played by Generals Faiz Mohammad, Kashmir Khan, and Commander Sabawon, all Kabul-based Hezb-e Islami commanders.

Jamiat, Shura-e Nazar, and the Afghan Government of 1992-1993

Jamiat and Shura-e Nazar forces, at the time discussed in this report, were under the overall command of Ahmed Shah Massoud (killed on September 9, 2001). Second tier military commanders included Mohammad Qasim Fahim (Afghanistan's defense minister 2001-2004; as of mid-2005 holding a symbolic position as "Marshall for Life"); Baba Jalander (director of the Afghan Red Crescent Society from late 2001-2004); Bismullah Khan (as of mid-2005 the chief of staff of the Afghan Army); Gul Haider (as of mid-2005 a general serving in the defense ministry); and Younis Qanooni (former minister of education and national security advisor in President Karzai's 2002-2004 cabinet; as of mid-2005 the chief of Nehzat-e Melli, a political party, also known as Afghanistan Naveen).

Middle level Jamiat commanders in Kabul included Baba Jan (as of mid-2005 the chief of police in Herat), General Abdul Momin (deceased), and Basir Salangi (chief of police in Kabul in 2003; as of mid-2005 chief of police in Wardak province), as well as other commanders Kabir Andarabi (until mid-2005 a senior ministry of defense commander, stationed in Bagrami; as of mid-2005 a police official in the ministry of interior), Haji Almas (parliamentary candidate and businessman; as of mid-2005 a senior commander in the ministry of defense, stationed in Parwan), Baz Mohammad Ahmadi (as of mid-2005 an official in the ministry of defense), Mullah Ezat (parliamentary candidate; as of 2005 a senior ministry of defense commander), Panah (reportedly deceased), and Anwar Dangar (joined the Taliban in 1996 and was killed in Peshawar in 2004).

Jamiat forces are culpable for many of the abuses documented in this report. There is compelling evidence that Jamiat forces in 1992 and 1993 intentionally targeted civilians and civilian areas in western Kabul for attack, or indiscriminately attacked such areas without distinguishing between civilian areas and military targets.

In some cases, Jamiat forces used imprecise weapons systems, including Sakr rockets and UB-16 and UB-32 S-5 airborne rocket launchers clumsily refitted onto tank turrets, the use of which was inherently indiscriminate in the dense urban setting. The use of the jury-rigged S-5 system in particular, within Kabul city, demonstrates an utter disregard of the duty to use methods and means of attack that distinguish between civilian objects and military targets.

There is also evidence that some Jamiat forces engaged in killing and abduction of Hazara civilians in 1992. There is also evidence that Jamiat forces targeted civilian areas for attack at the beginning of the February 1993 Afshar campaign. In addition, Jamiat commanders may in some cases be liable for the abuses committed during the Afshar campaign by allied Ittihad troops, if it is shown in any cases that they had de facto command over such troops. All of these alleged abuses amount to war crimes.

In addition, Jamiat, along with the other factions discussed in this report, are implicated in numerous robberies, general criminality, and killings of civilians in non-combat situations. Many of these abuses also amount to serious violations of international humanitarian law and human rights law, and the failures by commanders to stop or prevent the abuses could make them complicit in the violations.

Ahmad Shah Massoud is implicated in many of the abuses documented in this report, both those committed by Jamiat forces, and those committed by other militia forces under his command. He was assassinated on September 9, 2001. It is nonetheless important that his role and that of his commanders be fully investigated.

Further investigation is needed into the responsibility of Massoud's sub-commanders. Most of Massoud's commanders and advisors in 1992-1993 are still alive as of mid-2005, including Mohammad Qasim Fahim, Baba Jalander, Bismullah Khan, Gul Haider, Younis Qanooni, Dr. Abdullah, Baba Jan, Basir Salangi, Haji Almas, and Mullah Ezat (or Ezatullah). All of them hold or have held military or police posts in the post-Taliban Afghan government. (The official positions of Kabir Andarabi, Baz Mohammad Ahmadi, Ahmadi Takhari, and Panah are unknown.)

As stated in section III (A) and III (C), Fahim, Baba Jalander, Bismullah Khan, Baba Jan, Ahmadi Takhari, Kabir Andarabi, and Mullah Ezat were directly implicated in abuses described in this report, including the 1993 Afshar campaign. General Fahim was chief of the Afghan intelligence service and controlled several military posts in Kabul, and was one of the chief commanders under Massoud. As noted in section III (C), Fahim controlled at least one of the military posts on Television Mountain throughout the period covered in this report, was involved in the planning of the Afshar campaign and took part in negotiations with Harakat commanders to gain their cooperation before the attack, and was directly involved in the Afshar attack. Yunis Qanooni was stationed at the ministry of defense compound in Kabul, often served as a spokesman for Jamiat, and was involved in Jamiat decision-making processes. As noted in section III (C), Mullah Ezat and Anwar Dangar were also deeply involved in the Afshar attack.

According to the Afghan Justice Project, which researched the command structure of Jamiat during the Afshar assault, Fahim was responsible for "special operations in support of the offensive and participating in planning of the operation." Anwar Dangar and Mullah Ezat were named by numerous witnesses as "leading troops in Afshar that carried out abuses on the first two days of the operation." Baba Jalander also was reported to have "participated in the assault," along with Mohammad Ishaq Panshiri, Haji Bahlol Panshiri, Khanjar Akhund, Mushdoq Lalai, and Baz Mohammad Ahmadi Badakhshani.[309]

Several individuals who were Afghan government officials during the period covered in this report are also potentially implicated in the abuses. The sovereignty of Afghanistan during 1992-1993 was vested formally in "The Islamic State of Afghanistan." This government was headed from April to June 1992 by Sibghatullah Mujaddidi, and then held by Burhanuddin Rabbani, the political leader of Jamiat. Both men were involved in military decision-making processes during the period of this report, and should be further investigated to determine their potential culpability for abuses. As noted in section III (C) above, Rabbani was present at some decision-making meetings before the Afshar attack. His role relating to the commission of abuses during that attack should be investigated.

Junbish

Abdul Rashid Dostum, a former General in Soviet-backed Afghan army in the 1980's, was and is the overall leader of the Junbish party. (As of mid-2005 Dostum was serving as a senior general in the ministry of defense and was exercising significant political and

---

[309] AJP report, January 2005, p. 28.

military influence over several provinces in the north of Afghanistan. He also ran for president in the 2004 election.) Secondary Junbish commanders in 1992-1993 included Abdul Cherik (deceased), Majid Rouzi (a senior military official in the Junbish faction), Mohsin Homayun Fouzi (reportedly a senior official in the ministry of defense), Jura Beig (reportedly deceased), Rasul Pahlavan, Zeini Pahlavan, and Rahim Pahlavan.

Junbish, along with the other factions discussed in this report, are implicated in numerous murders, pillage, and looting. Many of these abuses amount to serious violations of international humanitarian law, and the failure by Junbish commanders to stop or prevent the abuses could make them responsible as a matter of command responsibility. (Junbish was also involved in numerous serious abuses in Kabul in 1994-1995, but this period is not the subject of this report.)

All of Junbish's main commanders should be investigated to determine their involvement in 1992-1993 abuses.

Harakat

The Harakat party, at the time of these abuses, was officially under the overall control of Mohammad Asef Mohseni, but its main military commanders were Hossein Anwari and Mohammad Ali Javeed (both members of President Karzai's interim cabinet, 2002-2004; Anwari was appointed governor of Kabul in 2005; Javeed is now the political leader of Harakat).

Harakat leaders, though not a primary force in the abuses documented in this report, are implicated in several cases where violations of international humanitarian law occurred. Investigation is needed into the role and specific legal responsibility of Harakat's commanders.

Afterword: The Complicity of Other Countries

The atrocities documented in this report did not occur in a vacuum. As noted in the introduction above, outside countries played a vital role in militarizing Afghanistan over the 1980s and fueling the political instability that plagued the country during 1992-1993, as well as in subsequent years.

Afghanistan was not hugely unstable, fractured, or militarized in 1978, when the Soviet Union orchestrated the communist coup in Kabul. But the decision of the Soviet Union in 1979 to invade and suppress the mujahedin uprising, and the Soviet Union's subsequent support for a series of brutal regimes through the 1980s, coupled with decisions by the United States, United Kingdom, Saudi Arabia, China, Iran, and Pakistan to support the mujahedin, ultimately made Afghanistan one of the most unstable, fractured, and militarized places in the world.

As noted earlier in this report, the Soviet Union spent approximately U.S. $36 to $48 billion to support successive Afghan regimes in the 1980s, while the other countries noted above sent roughly U.S. $6 to $12 billion in aid to mujahedin groups.[310] Even after the Soviet Union departed in 1989, the Soviet government continued to support the Najibullah government, and the United States and Pakistan continued to support mujahedin groups.[311] Hezb-e Islami forces continued to receive largescale military

---

[310] See Goodson, *Afghanistan's Endless War*, pp. 63 and 99; Coll, *Ghost Wars*, pp. 65-66, 151, 190, and 239. See generally, George Crile, *Charlie Wilson's War: The Extraordinary Story of the Largest Convert Operation in History* (New York: Atlantic Monthly Press, 2003); Human Rights Watch, *Crisis of Impunity: The Role of Pakistan, Russia, and Iran in Fueling the Civil War*, A Human Rights Watch Short Report, July 2001, vol. 13, no. 3 (C).

[311] For more on continued support by the United States, and on internal disputes between the U.S. State Department and CIA about the wisdom of such continued support, see Human Rights Watch World Report (1992), Afghanistan chapter, available at http://www.hrw.org/reports/1992/WR92/ASW-01.htm#P54_20418.

assistance from the United States and Pakistan through the early 1990s.[312] Wahdat and Harakat continued to receive funding from Iran though the 1990s.[313]

All of this military aid, training, and financial support—by the Soviet Union, United States, United Kingdom, Saudi Arabia, China, Pakistan, and Iran—provided these countries varying degrees of leverage over the armed groups they supported. All of these seven countries (including Russia in the case of the Soviet Union) share responsibility for the international crimes that occurred in Afghanistan during the period discussed in this report.

The weapons used in the atrocities documented in this report were sent to Afghanistan by these seven countries. These weapons sent were manufactured by the Soviet Union, the United States, China, and Pakistan. Much of the training on their use was conducted by trainers from Pakistan, Iran, the Soviet Union, the United States, and the United Kingdom. Moreover, the very fact that military force was being used in Afghanistan in 1992-1993 was in large part due to the fact that none of the seven countries above made any high-profile efforts to resolve the Afghan political situation after the collapse of the Soviet Union.

The governments of these seven countries today have an obligation to help Afghanistan rebuild and help it face its past. An important way to do so would be to forcefully and publicly press for justice for past crimes and support Afghan justice-building efforts.

---

[312] Ibid. As noted in the introduction, the CIA, with Pakistani support, sent new massive shipments of military aid to Hekmatyar in 1991, including large shipments of Soviet weapons and tanks captured from Saddam Hussein's forces during the first Gulf War. The aid was meant for his forces to use in an assault on Najibullah's forces in Kabul. The attack was called off, but the weapons were used later by Hekmatyar to attack Kabul in 1992-1995. See Coll, *Ghost Wars*, p. 226; and Steve Coll, "Afghan Rebels Said to Use Iraqi Tanks," *The Washington Post*, October 1, 1991.

[313] Human Rights Watch, "The Forgotten War: Human Rights Abuses and Violations of the Laws Of War Since the Soviet Withdrawal," A Human Rights Watch report, February 1991; Human Rights Watch, *Crisis of Impunity: The Role of Pakistan, Russia, and Iran in Fueling the Civil War*.

Recommendations

Afghans want justice for the crimes of the past. The Afghan Independent Human Rights Commission (AIHRC) completed an extensive survey in 2004, based on in-depth interviews and focus groups, addressing issues of justice and accountability for past abuses. The survey makes it clear that the vast majority of Afghans want the past to be confronted, do not see such efforts as destabilizing, and want justice sooner rather than later.

According to the AIHRC survey results, 94 percent of Afghans consider justice for past crimes to be either "very important" (75.9 percent) or "important" (18.5 percent). When asked what the effects would be for Afghanistan in bringing war criminals to justice, 76 percent said it would "increase stability and bring security," and only 7.6 percent said it would "decrease stability and threaten security." Almost half of those questioned said war criminals should be brought to justice "now," and another 25 percent said perpetrators should be tried "within two years."

Human Rights Watch, along with numerous other international and Afghan non-governmental organizations, has repeatedly called on Afghan officials and international actors involved in Afghanistan to help create mechanisms to hold persons responsible for major human rights abuses, war crimes, and crimes against humanity committed during Afghanistan's wars. We fully agree with the AIHRC on the need for this issue to receive more attention. We support their view that the president and government of Afghanistan should better prioritize justice for victims of past abuses and fully endorse efforts to hold perpetrators accountable.

Human Rights Watch therefore urges the government to accelerate efforts to create justice-seeking mechanisms to bring past abusers to justice and sideline them from political power and government positions. We urge the government to embrace justice and accountability as vital for the rule of law and the protection of human rights now and in the future.

We also urge the government, with the active support of donors, to accelerate reforms to the judicial system of Afghanistan, which are essential to successful justice-seeking efforts. The appointment of properly trained and independently-minded judges and prosecutors, who owe no allegiance to factional leaders or regional strongmen, is crucial. The president should take a leadership role in creating the conditions necessary for genuine judicial independence, chiefly by ensuring that government officials do not interfere in individual cases before the courts. The government and its donors must also prioritize efforts to create a well-educated legal profession.

Some will argue that pursuing justice for past crimes will create political instability, as many human rights abusers and potential defendants remain in power at both the national and regional levels.

We believe this threat is consistently overstated. There is always a risk in seeking justice against powerful individuals for the human rights abuses they commit. With the support of the international community and civil society, justice-seeking processes have been undertaken in similarly fragile post-conflict settings. And as noted above, the AIHRC survey has indicated that three in four Afghans believe that achieving justice for past crimes would increase stability, not decrease it.

Renewed respect for human rights and the rule of law can help to create sustainable stability in Afghanistan. A serious and successful accountability process is a key means towards this goal.

By contrast, one of the biggest threats to Afghanistan's political stability and future comes from individuals who have committed serious human rights abuses in the past. These are the people who are today most likely to resort to force and other extra-legal measures to circumvent and subvert Afghanistan's political process and legal system. To achieve long-term stability, the government will ultimately have to address the continuing threat from these individuals.

As an immediate first step, we recommend that the government implement a set of vetting processes for government officials, as specified in more detail below.

As detailed below, we also recommend that the government and key international actors work to create a Special Court to try past offenders. We recommend that the court be comprised of both Afghan and international judges, with an international majority, and that the prosecutor's office be led by an international prosecutor. If it proves impossible to establish the Special Court in Afghanistan, because of political opposition, lack of judicial independence or political impartiality, or problems related to security of witnesses or court personnel, we recommend that the court be physically located outside of the country.

We are aware of the domestic sensitivities to this second proposal and the legal and practical complexities of implementing it. Still, we believe there are several arguments for this approach that weigh in its favor. A Special Court, ideally located in Afghanistan but elsewhere if necessary, would have the best chance of meeting recognized fair trial standards. Such a court would also be better placed than a domestic court in the current environment to handle the complexities, both technical and political, of major trials.

But a Special Court, which will only take up a limited number of cases, will not be enough to address the enormity of Afghanistan's past abuses. For this reason, we further recommend that the president appoint a standing panel of high-level and independent Afghan and international experts to propose and help implement additional programs to address issues that are not dealt with by the Special Court, such as:

- Past crimes that the Special Court does not have the capacity to address or which fall outside of its jurisdiction;
- The establishment of an archive for the historical documentation of past abuses;
- Recommendations on appropriate restitution or compensation mechanisms; and
- Educational initiatives, such as the drafting of fair historical accounts in school textbooks.

Specific recommendations are as follows:

To the Afghan Government:

Civil Service and Political Appointments
- The president, provincial governors, and other public officials should not appoint to public office individuals who have had credible allegations made against them about the commission of serious violations of human rights and international humanitarian law or crimes against humanity. Appointed officials already in office who have had credible allegations made against them should be dismissed.
- Civil service applicants should be screened to reject applicants who have had credible allegations made against them about the commission of serious violations of human rights and international humanitarian law or crimes against humanity.
- Current civil servants who have had credible allegations made against them should be removed in accordance with civil service regulations. The civil service regulations should be amended as necessary to permit the removal of persons in such circumstances in keeping with due process guarantees, including the right to contest the claims through an impartial and independent process.

- The government should reform and strengthen the Civil Service Commission (CSC), as recommended by the AIHRC. Persons appointed to the CSC should be independent experts without direct links to military or political factions.

- The CSC should be empowered to hold both public hearings and receive confidential information on allegations concerning past criminal acts by those appointed to public office. CSC boards should maintain special mechanisms to allow women and girls to safely and confidentially provide information.

- Judgments on eligibility for office should not be based solely on past or present affiliations. Mere membership in a political party, military group, mujahedin militia, or government office, should not be considered a crime or abuse. Persons subject to removal from positions should have the opportunity to know the evidence against them, obtain a fair hearing before an impartial board, and have the right to appeal the determination of that tribunal to the regularly constituted courts.

- The AIHRC, along with established Afghan and international human rights groups, should be empowered to present evidence and bring complaints on behalf of victims and survivors of past abuses before the CSC.

- The CSC should have regional boards empowered to hold hearings in regional centers.

Candidates and Elected Officials

- In future election periods, Afghanistan's Electoral Commission should be empowered to hold public hearings at which allegations can be brought against candidates about their past serious human rights abuses, violations of international humanitarian law, and crimes against humanity, as well as violations of the electoral law and candidates legal qualifications. (Under 2005 election arrangements, the Electoral Commission worked in cooperation with a U.N. component to hear complaints about candidates, but only about allegations of violations of the electoral law and candidates' legal qualifications.)

- The AIHRC should be empowered to present evidence and bring complaints before the Electoral Commission on behalf of victims and survivors of past abuses. Persons alleged to have committed abuses should be given an opportunity to rebut charges and submit evidence.

- The Electoral Commission should issue a public report on the evidence presented. The Electoral Commission should forward all reports to the Attorney General's office for possible criminal investigation.

- The Electoral Commission should create regional boards empowered to hold hearings in regional centers.

- In accordance with the Afghan constitution, future Electoral Commissions should enforce provisions that bar any candidates or elected officials who have been convicted of crimes against humanity or other criminal acts, or sentenced by a court to the deprivation of their civil rights.

- The future parliament should work to formulate legislation defining the work of the Electoral Commission and the terms of its mandate.

Criminal Prosecutions

- To address crimes committed under international and domestic law during the armed conflicts in Afghanistan since 1978, the government should establish a Special Court, empowered to investigate and prosecute war crimes, crimes against humanity, and other serious human rights crimes.

- The Special Court should be empowered to prosecute individuals on the basis of Afghan law in effect at the time of the offense as well as applicable international law, including international humanitarian law, international law regarding crimes against humanity, and other relevant international criminal law.

- The Special Court must be independent and impartial and meet international fair trial standards. It should include an effective protection program for victims and witnesses and their families. Due to domestic sensitivities and the deep social stigma associated with sexual violence in Afghanistan, the Special Court should create confidential, anonymous, and secure mechanisms for women and girls to present evidence on sexual abuses.

- Because the Afghan criminal justice system is currently incapable of investigating and prosecuting complex international crimes, and because of practical difficulties in guaranteeing that such a court would be impartial if domestically administered, the Special Court should be a mixed court comprised of both Afghan and international judges and prosecutors. To guard against political manipulation by powerful individuals who may be targets of criminal investigations, the court should have a majority of international judges and a prosecutor's office led by an international prosecutor. The government should work with the future parliament to address legal and constitutional issues arising from its creation. If necessary, the government should seek to amend the Afghan Constitution to address these issues.

- The AIHRC should be empowered to bring complaints to the prosecutor of the Special Court on behalf of victims and survivors.

- The creation of a Special Court should be coordinated with broader efforts to improve and expand the criminal justice system in Afghanistan and to ensure compliance with international due process standards.

- The government should grant no amnesties or other immunities to persons implicated in war crimes, crimes against humanity, or other serious violations of international human rights law. There must be no exceptions for government officials.

- To address any future crimes of this magnitude and to bring Afghanistan into conformity with its treaty obligations, the government should implement the Rome Statute of the International Criminal Court, ratified by Afghanistan in 2003. After the parliamentary elections scheduled for late 2005, the president should immediately propose legislation to the new parliament that would criminalize, under Afghan law, war crimes, crimes against humanity, genocide, and other serious violations of human rights. The president should work with the new parliament to enact additional legislation as required by the Rome Statute.

Other Mechanisms

- The president should appoint a standing panel of high-level and independent Afghan and international experts to propose and help implement additional programs and policies to address those aspects of Afghanistan's history of abuse that are not dealt with by the Special Court. This should include an archive for the historical documentation of past abuses, recommendations on appropriate restitution or compensation mechanisms, and undertaking educational initiatives, such as the drafting of fair historical accounts in school textbooks.

To International Actors and Donors:

- International actors and donors should offer political, technical, and financial support to efforts to establish the accountability mechanisms discussed in the above recommendations.
- International actors should take into account public opinion in Afghanistan in formulating policies about past crimes and accountability mechanisms.
- Other countries should fully cooperate with investigations into past abuses, including by allowing access to documents and other materials held outside Afghanistan.

Appendix

Jamiat-e Islami-yi Afghanistan (Jamiat)[314]

Jamiat was one of the original Islamist parties in Afghanistan, established in the 1970s by students at Kabul University, where its leader, Burhanuddin Rabbani, was a lecturer in the Islamic Law Faculty. Although Rabbani was the official head of Jamiat through the 1980s and early 1990s, the most powerful figure within the party was Ahmad Shah Massoud, who led the military wing of Jamiat-e Islami through the 1980s. (Massoud was assassinated on September 9, 2001.) Rabbani is Tajik, as was Massoud, and Jamiat-e Islami was and remains a predominately Tajik party. Rabbani has a base of support in the northeast province of Badakhshan. Massoud's ethnic power base was historically in Parwan and Takhar provinces, where he established a regional military and administrative structure in the late 1980s, the Supervisory Council of the North (Shura-e Nazar). Rabbani became the President of Afghanistan in 1992, and the government under his control was predominately comprised of Jamiat members. Mohammad Qasim Fahim, Abdullah, and Yunis Qanooni—all members of President Hamid Karzai's interim cabinet from 2002-2004—were members of Jamiat and Shura-e Nazar.

Ittihad-i Islami Bara-yi Azadi Afghanistan (Ittihad)[315]

Ittihad is headed by Abdul Rabb al-Rasul Sayyaf. During the war against the Soviet occupation, Sayyaf obtained considerable assistance from Saudi Arabia, and Arab volunteers supported by private and governmental sources from Saudi Arabia fought with Sayyaf's forces. Ittihad in 1992-1993 had its central power based in Paghman district, west of Kabul, and was allied with the Rabbani government and Massoud's Jamiat forces. Today, Sayyaf has no official government post but exercises a large amount of political power of President Karzai's political, judicial, and military appointments. Many Ittihad members have served from 2002 to mid-2005 as officials in the ministry of defense, ministry of interior, and in the Supreme Court and lower courts.

Hezb-e Wahdat-e Islami-yi Afghanistan (Wahdat)[316]

The principal Shi'a party in Afghanistan with support mainly among the Hazara ethnic community, Hezb-e Wahdat was originally formed by Abdul Ali Mazari to unite eight Shi'a parties in Afghanistan in the run-up to the collapse of the communist government.

---

[314] *Jamiat-e Islami-yi Afghanistan* means "Islamic Society of Afghanistan."

[315] *Ittihad-i Islami Bara-yi Azadi Afghanistan* means "Islamic Union for the Liberation of Afghanistan."

[316] *Hezb-e Wahdat-e Islami-yi Afghanistan* means "Islamic Unity Party of Afghanistan."

Mazari was Wahdat's leader in 1992-1993, but its senior commanders also included Muhammad Karim Khalili and Haji Muhammad Muhaqqiq, who commanded troops in Kabul and in the north of Afghanistan at the time. Hezb-e Wahdat received significant military support from Iran in the early 1990s. Mazari was killed in 1995, as the Taliban were fighting to seize Kabul. Both Khalili and Muhaqqiq were members of President Karzai's cabinet in 2002-2004 and Khalili was elected as a vice-president in the October 2004 election.

Junbish-e Milli-yi Islami-yi Afghanistan (Junbish)[317]

Junbish brought together northern ethnic Uzbek and Turkmen militias of the communist regime who mutinied against President Najibullah in early 1992. It also included former leaders and administrators of the old regime from various other ethnic groups, mainly Persian-speaking, and some Uzbek mujahedin commanders, as well as some erstwhile Jamiat and Wahdat commanders who later left Junbish and rejoined their former factions. This group took control of the important northern city of Mazar-i Sharif in alliance with Jamiat in early 1992 and controlled much of the northern provinces of Samangan, Balkh, Jowzjan, Faryab, and Baghlan provinces. The leader of Junbish throughout the 1990s and up to the present is Abdur Rashid Dostum, who ran for president in the 2004 election.

Harakat-e Islami-yi Afghanistan (Harakat)[318]

Harakat-e Islami was a Shi'a political party and mujahedin force founded in the early 1980s. The Harakat-e Islami party was headed for most of the 1980s by a Shi'a cleric named Mohammad Asef Mohseni (who participated in the June 2002 loya jirga). Over the last decade, Harakat-e Islami has splintered into three parts. One faction is led by the original leader, Mohammad Asef Mohseni, a second splinter is led by a military commander Hossein Anwari (agricultural minister in Afghanistan's transitional government and in mid-2005 the governor of Kabul), and a third is led by Sayeed Mohammad Ali Javeed (until 2004 the minister of transportation). In 1992-1993, Harakat received substantial support from Iran. But although predominately Shi'a, Harakat never joined the Wahdat party.

---

[317] *Junbish-e Milli-yi Islami-yi Afghanistan* means "National Islamic Movement of Afghanistan."

[318] *Harakat-e Islami-yi Afghanistan* means "Islamic Movement of Afghanistan."

Acknowledgements

This report is based on research conducted by Human Rights Watch researchers in 2003 through 2005 in Afghanistan and from New York. Brad Adams, Executive Director of the Asia Division and Joe Saunders, Deputy Program Director, edited the report. James Ross, Senior Legal Advisor, provided legal review. Nisha Varia, Zama Coursen-Neff, and Marc Garlasco also reviewed the report and provided comments. Jo-Anne Prud'homme, Ami Evangelista, Liz Weiss, Angelina Fisher, and Jane Stratton provided research assistance.

Production assistance was provided by Veronica Matushaj, Andrea Holley, Fitzroy Hepkins, and Jagdish Parikh. John Emerson designed the map. Human Rights Watch would like to thank Space Imaging for their generous contribution of satellite imagery of Kabul. Matthew McKenzie designed the satellite photograph images.

Human Rights Watch specially thanks the Afghan women and men whom we interviewed for this report and who assisted us in our investigation. For security reasons, many of them cannot be named here.

We would also like to thank the countless staff and officials of non-governmental organizations and U.N. agencies in Afghanistan who have assisted us with our work, as well as the numerous other sources who provided helpful comments, advice, and information. We want to specially thank international and Afghan television, radio, and print journalists who have provided information for this report.

We would also like to thank Ahmed Rashid for his support and encouragement, as well as Barnett R. Rubin and Patricia Gossman for their ongoing assistance.

Our work on Afghanistan has required significant financial resources. We thank the Ford Foundation, the John D. and Catherine T. MacArthur Foundation, the Carnegie Corporation of New York, Stichting Doen, and Rockefeller Brothers Fund for their generous contributions to our emergency work in Afghanistan in 2003.

We also wish to acknowledge the generous support of the Annenberg Foundation, which has enabled Human Rights Watch to sustain our monitoring of Afghanistan.